The 1930s and 1940s
...Pain and Pleasure

Wendell Trogdon

An Eyewitness to History

Backroads Press
P.O. Box 651
Mooresville IN 46158

ISBN 0-9724033-1-0

Cover by Gary Varvel

Printed by Country Pines, Inc.
Shoals, Indiana
USA

DEDICATION

This book is a tribute to my long-deceased parents who taught me the values of fairness, faith, friendship and work, to my wife who has made sure I lived by those virtues and to my children who have followed them. It also is a testimonial to all the men and women who have shared their wisdom with me for over 70-plus years. I thank each of them.

ACKNOWLEDGMENTS

Numerous sources were checked in our research for this book, among them *The Bedford Times-Mail* and former newspapers like *The Indianapolis News, Bedford Daily Mail* and *The Bedford Daily Times*. The late Jim Guthrie's *A Quarter Century in Lawrence County (1917-1941)* was helpful as were numerous Internet sites. My previous *Those Were The Days* books revived my memories of many incidents. A number of individuals have offered their recollections.

Some readers no doubt will have different recollections and recall personal experiences. We expect them to and will be delighted if this book awakens forgotten incidents from their pasts.

CONTENTS

OVERVIEW

Each of us is shaped by our youth and tempered by our environment. Our mettle is forged by the rigors we face and toughened by the challenges we confront.

The depression of the 1930s and the war of the 1940s was for many the worst of times. For a farm boy it was—looking through the rearview mirror of life—the best of times to learn to cope with life's inevitable challenges.

Those decades were our classrooms onto the world. We saw the drama of survival under duress, the contrast between the darkness of hardships and the sunshine of happiness. We viewed from a distance the conflict between nations and peoples, between tyranny and freedom.

The two decades saw Americans accept social welfare programs, unaware they would become a permanent part of the nation's psyche.

The economic woes of the 1930s were global, few parts of the world exempt. Economic distress led to political uncertainty in most nations. Political disorder led to the rise of Adolf Hitler in Germany, allowed the Fascisti party of Benito Mussolini to remain in power in Italy and brought the military to power in Japan. Each of those nations would soon seek to widen their regimes and broaden their domains.

We have chosen incidents from our past to relate part of the history of that era, not for personal attention but because they were similar to the experiences of much of rural America at that time.

We chose to be products, not victims, of our circumstances. We were unaware of wealth, power, prestige or influence for we had none so we knew not what we missed. Life was not a daily hardship, it was a blessing, an experience to be savored. The hills and hollows were our laboratories, our nature centers; our barns and farm fields places to learn the value of work, the care and feeding of animals and the pursuit of victory in endless games of basketball.

We were privileged to be sons of the soil, although it would be years before we recognized opportunities our lives offered us. We often felt inferior to kids in town, who seemed to dress better, wore shoes free of farm dirt, were exempt from outdoor chores, could walk to the movies and lived in homes with electricity and indoor plumbing.

Our lives were simple. We awakened each morning, the smell of fresh bacon and sausage asizzle on the wood-fired kitchen stove, ate hearty meals, milked cows, fed the livestock, curried the draft horses and separated cream from the milk. Yet somehow we always were ready for school when the bus arrived.

At times that part of our life seems another existence away. At times it is as fresh as today, as vivid as a sunrise over the winter snow.

We would have had that background no other way, even if that had been possible.

We are grateful to have grown up in the environment, and in the era, we did.

QUIET TIME

July 23, 1929, is not a date that lives in infamy or in history. Page One of the *Bedford Daily Times* that day was devoted almost entirely to national Associated Press reports of little relevance to Lawrence County readers.

The lead story reported President Herbert Hoover had named a commission to see what could be done to reduce military expenditures. Little did readers know that military costs would reach record numbers in the decade to come and be a subject for endless debates into the 21st Century.

Another Page 1 story noted a Bedford woman's suit for divorce which was news at the time because legal separations were rare and often frowned on by churches and society in general. Such cases would soon become so common they were seldom mentioned in newspapers except in agate type amid court proceedings.

Inside pages were filled with personal items for it was an era when neighbors had time to be interested in each other and curious about their neighbors. Among the items were a report a Bedford boy had his tonsils removed and a mention that a Bedford man had visited his daughter in Bloomfield just an hour or so away.

Ribble's Market offered margarine, uncolored, for 15 cents a pound, sugar cured ham and beef roast each for 18 cents a pound. A car dealer offered a used 1927 Whippet, a favorite among farm families, for $375.

The date is mentioned only as a point of reference. It was the date of my birth, which was, as most were, at home not in a hospital maternity ward.

Years later when I sought a birth certificate, instead of my first name, I was identified as "Infant Boy Trogdon." Dr. Jasper Cain, who made the house call, had left our home without waiting to hear what name my parents had chosen.

The place of birth was Pleasant Run Township, northeastern Lawrence County, Indiana, the mail address Norman in Jackson County, which with Heltonville would be the centers of our childhood universe.

I could have chosen any first name to enter the world of work, "Infant Baby Trogdon," likely inappropriate to most employers. I kept the name Wendell that my mom had written in the family Bible that July day in 1929.

"Doc" Cain would become a friend, one who would remain so until his death when I was a pallbearer at his funeral. He will be mentioned again.

GREAT DEPRESSION

An event of October 24, 1929, was scarcely noted by small town newspapers.

It was a date that would become known as Black Friday for investors of the stock market. *The New York Times* index of 50 stocks fell from 261.97 to 255.39 points, a mere 2.5 percent drop, but one that sent a seismic tremor across the economic world.

It was of little concern at the time for most Americans. Families of modest means kept what extra cash they had in banks. Most stocks were owned by the wealthy, unlike in later years when most households would own at least a few shares.

The date, however, would be linked to the Great Depression, an era that, in fact, contained two recessions. One that began almost unnoticed is said to have lasted from August, 1929, to March, 1933. Production of goods and service fell by 36 to 42 percent. A period of slight recovery followed until another recession from May, 1937, to June 1939, saw a 6 to 9 percent drop in production.

The Great Depression would change America forever. It brought a wave of crime, bank closings, migrations of people across the nation and financial hardships for millions.

In the years ahead President Franklin Delano Roosevelt would introduce social engineering to politics, create a host of federal agencies with alphabetic names and use make-work programs to employ the jobless. Government would begin to do for citizens what they could not do for themselves.

To a degree FDR was successful. Social Security became a financial blanket, roads were built, parks were developed and hope replaced despair.

But he also brought a philosophy that sapped the nation of its rugged individualism and made government a Big Brother who would always be at our side, whether we would want him there or not.

The Great Depression, world-wide and severe, would dominate the news for the rest of the decade and impact our lives as it would every other American.

Newspapers reported in 1932 the invention of air conditioning, which held little meaning for farm families whose homes were without electricity and residents of cities and towns who had no money to install such a convenience.

Those who that year read that scientists had split the atom had no idea of its implications. The introduction of the Zippo lighter would mean more to most folks, especially smokers.

THE ROOSEVELT YEARS

Democrat Franklin D. Roosevelt swept to victory over President Herbert Hoover in the 1932 election, winning all but a few states and 472 of 531 electoral votes.

The vote climaxed a campaign that centered on the Great Depression. Hoover painted Roosevelt as an extremist who would ruin the America voters knew. Roosevelt campaigned vigorously for economic reform, his effort exhausting despite the effects of polio which had stricken him years earlier.

Voters, citing the unemployment of 25 percent of the work force, chose the New York governor in hopes of an economic recovery.

Roosevelt took office in 1933 and told the nation in his inaugural address "the only thing we have to fear is fear itself." That fear, he said, was "nameless, unreasoning, unjustified terror." A majority of Americans were confident in his promise of a "New Deal."

Fear was, indeed rampant. An estimated 13,000,000 Americans were jobless and most banks were closed. Urged by Roosevelt, Congress voted to enact programs in an effort to revive business and agriculture, bring relief to the unemployed and prevent foreclosure of mortgages on homes and farms.

*   *   *

My dad would tell me later he voted for Roosevelt, a man he would derisively in the years ahead call "The Great White Father." He would never again vote for him.

15

Roosevelt's programs did lead to jobs for many Americans. They also put the alphabet to work to identify numerous "make work" agencies.

Dozens of programs were known by initials, the first RFC, the Reconstruction Finance Corporation created by Hoover. Its job was to issue loans to distressed banks and corporations, but it would soon be another bureaucracy used by politicians for their own interests.

Others followed under Roosevelt. The FERA was the Federal Emergency Relief Administration, the CWA was the Civil Works Administration, the NRA was the National Recovery Act, the WPA was the Works Progress Administration soon called We Piddle Around by skeptics who claimed workers often loafed on their jobs.

Recreation directors, paid by the federal government, organized baseball teams, directed basketball and other sports for girls, and provided recreational opportunities for youngsters in rural areas. Most farm youths were too busy with daily chores to participate but we did envy those we sometimes watched play baseball games on a scraped wheat field.

By 1934, the economy was on a slight upturn. The Gross National Product rose by 7.7 percent and unemployment had dropped a few percentage points to 21.7.

A few families could buy a new board game called Monopoly that had been introduced by Parker Brothers.

Football fans found money to watch Columbia beat Stanford, 7-0, in the Rose Bowl and Duquesne routed Miami, 33-7, in the Orange Bowl. On January 7, 1934, Rev. Dr. William Ashley Sunday, better known as Billy Sunday, began a revival campaign in New York City.

And the "New Deal" continued to expand. Less criticized than most other agencies was the CCC, the Civilian Conservation Corps, which gave uniformed young men from 17 to 23 a sense of purpose, room and board and $30 a month. In return the workers helped reforest much of Indiana's hill country, build trails and improved state parks.

Their legacies still are rooted in trails in Spring Mill and other state parks and in the pine trees that anchor once eroded hills. Unknown to Roosevelt at the time, the CCC also would accustom the men to regimentation and discipline of the military service to which they were destined.

Some farmers accepted benefits of the AAA, the Agriculture Adjustment Act. Designed to regulate production, it also adjusted how much of what crop could be planted.

Independent and stubborn my dad disdained government interference. More than once he derided AAA agents who came to our house, maps of fields rolled under arm, to enroll him in whatever program was current. He was even more adamant when AAA workers showed up to stake our fields, telling the men, "I don't need them damned maps to tell me how many acres are in my fields." More than one left, using his figures, the maps they carried never unrolled.

"Doggone government didn't buy this land. I did," he said, having earned the money to buy it by shucking corn throughout winters in Iowa and northern Indiana and later as a diamond sawyer at mills in Indiana's limestone belt.

Dad had his allies, but they were in the minority. Numerous court cases were filed throughout the country against AAA programs. The opposition was outnumbered and outfinanced by a government which grew larger by the day.

As the nation gained relief from the recovery programs, some businessmen and bankers also turned against what Roosevelt called his "New Deal" program. FDR ignored his critics and endorsed new programs, seeking the enactment of Social Security, heavier taxes on the wealthy, new controls over banks and more work programs for the unemployed.

My first encounter with a WPA crew came in the winter of 1935. As a first grader I waited in freezing air beside the gravel road for our school bus. It was a relief when WPA workers assigned to clean the ditches at roadside welcomed me to join them around a steel drum red from the fire that burned inside.

It didn't bother me if they seemed to spend more time around the fire than in the ditches. But Dad scoffed when I told him, "It's good to know they are good for something."

One federal program did meet Dad's approval and led to the creation of the Hoosier National Forest which remains a southern Indiana asset. Overfarmed, much of the hilly terrain had eroded, leading the Indiana Legislature to ask Roosevelt to help preserve the forests that remained. He directed the U.S. Forestry Service to buy huge tracts of land that were replanted by CCC workers starting in 1935.

We often saw CCC crews at work in those days. We were pleased when the men created a swimming pool above a dam they built at the head of Henderson Creek west of Norman. That area is now overgrown, hidden by vegetation, only a memory to those who enjoyed it. The Hoosier National Forest, however, remains a part of the area's allure.

So do a few "Roosevelt Toilets," built by Civil Works crews in the mid-1930s under a Community Sanitation Project. Labor was free, homeowners paid for the materials.

The outhouses were refined compared to most outdoor privies built of makeshift lumber, one or two-holers a few feet above ground. A FDR toilet had a concrete floor and a deep pit sided with concrete that rarely needed to be emptied.

They were sources of pride and comfort to their owners, the butt, excuse the word, of others less fortunate.

Government-paid employees rebuilt streets, cleared debris from streams, erected buildings, installed storm drains and small dams and built sidewalks. Others directed music classes and writing projects for would-be authors. An "education department" for adults taught music, gardening, library and library administration.

The New Deal was a smorgasbord of programs too vast to be administered with efficiency and without criticism.

It was normal for low-paid workers with jobs in the private sector to resent the attention given to—and the public funds paid to—the unemployed, especially when they were seen resting against the handles of shovels.

It also led the *Bedford Daily Mail* to write in an editorial: "We don't blame the men for what they do, because there is no future or incentive in a WPA laborer's job. The average worker would much rather be employed at gainful labor at his old job, but the limestone industry at its lowest ebb . . . it is impossible for him to do so.

"It is absolutely common knowledge that the whole WPA relief system has been one of the poorest managed farces that ever existed. The executives and foremen in most instances were selected, not for their ability to handle men, but because of their political affiliations. They don't care whether the laborers work or not, and they are the ones to blame—not the workers—no matter what stories are told."

A Second Term

In November, Roosevelt, despite his critics, won a second term, defeating Republican Alf Landon of Kansas by a margin even wider than his 1932 victory over Herbert Hoover.

FDR carried 46 of the 48 states, losing only Maine and Vermont, receiving 60.8 percent of the popular vote and winning the electoral vote by a record 523-8 margin. A reported 56.9 percent of the eligible voters cast ballots. It was an amazing turnout compared to the number of Americans who would show up at the polls at the turn of the millennium.

Despite the support for the New Deal, a report in 1937 claimed the average family income in Lawrence County was $1,700 a year, with the debt per person $1,375. If there was money around it was in the hands of a few.

On February 5, 1937, FDR sought to widen his jurisdiction. "Roosevelt seeks control of Supreme Court," read newspaper headlines. The president had misread the 1936 election as a mandate. His move to expand his power would be one of his few political miscalculations.

His move to add justices to the high court came after the existing nine members declared the National Recovery Administration, the Agricultural Adjustment Act and the National Labor Relations Board unconstitutional.

Justices were appointed for life. He could have a majority vote of the court only by adding judges who held his views. He failed in that attempt and the court would continue to have nine members. The only result of his miscalculation was the alienation of even more voters.

Recession Amid Depression

Despite the New Deal's make work programs, the January 15, 1937, edition of the *Bedford Daily Times* listed eight pages of delinquent property taxes. A vast majority of the delinquent taxpayers were not deadbeats, but honest men and women caught in the grips of the depression.

By the summer of 1938, unemployment, which had dropped to 16.9 percent, had risen again to 19 percent. It would fall the next year, but mainly because the Roosevelt administration had borrowed $1 billion to build its armed forces as World War II appeared on the horizon.

FDR's foes would forever claim World War II ended the Great Depression, not his social welfare programs. Those programs, however, had given aid to millions, built parks and given hope when there was none to the hopeless. They provided a guide to offset severe economic recessions in the years ahead.

Its broadest and most lasting impact was the Social Security Administration, which affects almost each of us. It remains a source of debate today, both as to its future and its funding.

Government had changed as did how Americans came to look at it. It was now a Big Brother, benevolent, yet demanding, one who gives but also expects more for what it does.

In the end, however, America's biggest asset was the will of its people. As Ma Joad noted in *"Grapes of Wrath,"* the movie: "We're the people who live. They can't wipe us out. They can't lick us. We'll go on forever, Pa, cause we're the people."

Lawrence W. Levine, in an essay for "Documenting America: 1935 to 1943," wrote about Americans, "They also continued, as people always must, the business of living. They ate and they laughed, they loved and they fought, they worried and they hoped, they created and reared children, they worked and they played, they dressed and shopped and ate and bathed and watched movies and ball games and each other; they filled their days, as we fill ours, with the essentials of everyday living."

Meeting the Challenge

Farm families, like ours, survived better than those who lived in cities. We had a huge garden, some fruit trees, milked our cows, raised hogs for pork and steers for beef, traded eggs for staples with the huckster truck driver, sold butter and cream for some extra cash and cut wood for the kitchen range and heating stove.

Our cellar had enough filled canning jars to feed a family five time larger.

My brother, Wayne, and I found ways to make spending money. Dad showed us how to dig roots used for medications and took us to town to sell it to a dealer. He would laugh when we bragged we had dug what we thought was 30 pounds of Mayapple root, not knowing, once dried out, it would shrink to no more than three pounds and earn us a quarter if we were lucky. We occasionally cracked walnuts and hickory nuts and sold the kernels. We could have distributed *The Grit*, a weekly tabloid, but a neighbor already had a route through the area.

We sold zinc from canning jar lids and scrap iron to the junk man who stopped by occasionally. That went well until we sold an old harrow to Dad's chagrin. What he called "a perfectly good harrow" had not been used in years and its absence would not have been noticed if we had not told him what we had done.

Our first full-time job came when I was 10 as I recall.

Uncle Joe Cummings had a stationary hay baler which meant alfalfa or red clover was brought to the gasoline engine-operated baler where it was fed through a chute to be pressed into bales. I punched the wires though an opening in the block and Wayne tied them on the opposite side. While I replaced the block in the baler Wayne stacked the bale off to the side, a routine we followed for eight, sometimes ten hours. Joe paid us each $1.50 a day and we were delighted. Had it been a half-century later a do-gooder might have complained we were victims of child labor.

One Saturday Wayne and I sped to the home of an aging neighbor who had set fire to a patch of broomsage which quickly spread out of control. We used wet burlap bags that grew heavier with each swing to extinguish the flames in an effort to save a rail fence. We succeeded, saving all but a single section, coughing smoke as we savored victory.

The farmer paid us for his gratitude with a quarter each.

Back home, fuming and fiery of tongue, we told Dad he ought to demand Ben provide a bigger reward for our efforts. He shook his head. "Being a good neighbor doesn't come with a price," he explained, then added, "And you both look too tired to spend even a quarter anyhow." He was correct on both counts.

Cash for our first bicycles came in the mid-1930s from the sale of a hog Dad had given each of us. The two barrows were among a shipment of hogs sold at the stockyards. We received $15, or about 7.5 cents a pound for our hogs, after a neighbor was paid to haul the animals to Indianapolis and a commission firm paid to sell them to a meat packer. We griped about the deductions, which were, as we were to learn, normal for most business transactions.

I found the bike I wanted, an American Flyer, at Bill's Consolidated store on the square in Bedford. The price was $14.95, that being long before lawmakers dreamed up sales taxes to raise revenue.

Despite the joblessness elsewhere, Dad often worked nights at the stone mill. If he needed money to plant crops in the spring, he would ask the Stone City Bank in Bedford for a three-month loan, which he paid back when the wheat was threshed. It was a time when banks in county seats were locally-owned and officers knew customers as individuals not by account numbers.

Other men hewed crossties with double-bit axes and sold them to railroads. Others found work wherever they could. Most rural families cut their own wood for kitchen ranges and heating stoves, which were often shaped from 55-gallon steel drums.

All "made do," as they called it, the best they could. Few griped about their plight. All strived to play the cards the depression had dealt them.

Some friends across the way lived in a house built of unplaned lumber, the inside walls papered with newspapers. What other visitors might think tacky, we appreciated having the comics strips and news reports to read when conversation lulled.

We likely were poor, but we did not know it. We were not, however, immune to the hardships of others less fortunate.

Again and Again

President Roosevelt would be elected for two more terms, the first—and last—president to do so. Congress would vote later for a two-consecutive term limit.

He defeated Hoosier Wendell Willkie, "the barefoot boy from Wall Street," in the 1940 election when the GOP challenger polled a record number of votes (up to that time) for a losing candidate. Many of those votes were cast by the disenchanted and opponents of a third term for FDR.

Willkie called Rushville home even though he was more attuned to New York at the time. He later wrote "One World," which won him praise and criticism, which still is normal for would-be policy makers of today.

By September 17, 1941, the economy, aided by employment in defense plants, showed a 50 percent reduction in the number of jobless over the previous year. The cost of relief programs had dropped to the lowest point since pre-Depression 1929.

In 1944, Roosevelt defeated Tom Dewey, the New York governor. Dewey carried Indiana by 80,000 votes which my dad said proved that Hoosiers had more sense than voters in most states.

FDR chose Harry S Truman, a former U.S. senator from Missouri, as his vice presidential candidate. Truman's selection would prove to be an important decision.

PROHIBITION ENDS

Despite the economy, December 5, 1933, was a night for much of the nation to celebrate. Those who enjoyed alcoholic beverages cheered an Associated Press report that read:

"Tried for almost 14 years and adjudged wanting, constitutional prohibition ends tonight and the American people face a new period of experimentation on how to handle liquor."

The dry years had created a growth industry for some entrepreneurs in our area. Stills were common during—and after—prohibition producing hard liquor called "white lightning."

Moonshiners chose remote locations hidden far off narrow county roads for their operations, turning cheap corn into a liquid asset. The booze was in big demand. Runners from Chicago and other cities were said to drive high-powered cars with enough speed to outrun the police.

When adults saw an expensive car free of the red clay of Lawrence County roads they knew it was headed for a buy at a still. Many of the cars bore Illinois license tags and were said to carry cargo for the mobs in Chicago.

Times were hard and few men who favored prohibition criticized those who produced the liquor. Stills continued to operate throughout the area despite repeal of the 18th Amendment.

Revenuers did not stop the illegal production, which continued until World War II, but they did make a few arrests, including one operator who supposedly boasted his grain crops produced "two gallons an acre."

Teens from our youth recall the stories we heard when a neighbor was arrested at his "distillery." Despite his speech impediment when his arm was grabbed from behind by a lawman, he stammered through a profanity that ended with, "Watch it you damned fool, you'll make me spill part of my profit." His profit would have been the white lightning he was pouring into a quart Mason jar.

He was sent prison for a while, but no one called it that. Not wanting to disparage a neighbor, adults said he had been "sent away for a spell." Sent away meant a trip to the State Farm near Putnamville, as I recall. Condemnation was for the courts and for the All Mighty, not for them.

It must have been that man's still that a friend and I had seen a few days earlier amid briers and bushes on a wooded hillside. Even though no one was around, we were too scared to walk too close. I recall seeing some copper tubing, what looked like a makeshift wood stove, a few big drum-type barrels and some contorted copper tubing. A scent of mash reminded me of the residue from a Louisville distillery that was delivered to our home and fed to the hogs as slop.

We did not mention our find even to our parents.

No serious attempt has been made again to ban the sale of alcoholic beverages on a national scale.

WORLD WAR II

Amid depression, prohibition and a myriad of other concerns, Americans paid little heed to a news report from Berlin on January 1, 1933: "Nazi Adolf Hitler today was named chancellor of Germany in exchange for his political support of Paul von Hindenburg for president."

Hitler looked more like a cartoon character than a world leader, his gestures more similar to a mime than a statesman, but his oratory galvanized his support and sent fear to those who paid attention to his intent to conquer the world.

Hindenburg died 19 months later and Hitler became the consensus choice to lead the nation. He took credit for an improving economy, eliminated challenges from other political groups and cemented his self-assumed role as dictator. By 1934 he had established the first Nazi concentration camp.

The United States and much of the world remained in recession and in isolation from the implications and cruelty of the evilness of the Fuhrer's regime.

We lived in isolated rural Indiana and where most adults were too concerned with their own lives to read much about events in Germany.

Warning Ignored

Crime, depression and the weather dominated the news in the summer of 1934 but there were omens, perhaps even more distressing than the rise of Hitler, in other parts of the world.

U.S. Representative E.B. Crowe, a Democrat from Bedford, returned from a visit to Hawaii and warned a gathering in his home town that the island territory was almost defenseless.

Pearl Harbor's defense, he said, relied on howitzers which were old even before World War I. The Japanese, he observed, would have no trouble taking the islands. Crowe would continue to be critical of Hawaii's defense in the years ahead. No one in power in Washington paid enough attention to do anything about it.

Seven years later the nation would pay the consequences.

*   *   *

Fascisti Party Blackshirts marched into Rome in 1922 leading to the rule of Benito Mussolini. In 1934, his Italian Army invaded Ethiopia as it sought to extend its rule over Africa. Two years later Mussolini and Hitler gave their support to Fascists nationalists in the Spanish Civil War.

Gathering Storm

On January 8, 1937, President Roosevelt ordered the Navy to begin immediate construction of two battleships. The Associated Press story, however, hinted of no pending threat against the nation.

By November 1937, unknown to most folks in our area, Hitler's regime had built a military force that was primed for war and made him confident he could complete the master plan he had outlined in his book, "Mein Kampf." He presented his plans for world domination at what was called the "Fuhrer Conference," dismissing any objectors.

That same year, Japan, threatening peace in the Far East, invaded China. The world would soon know the consequences it faced from the opposite sides of the globe.

On March 1938, German troops crossed the border into Austria and soon annexed the nation. The Third Reich would extend its domination that year into the Sudetenland, a country that bordered Ethiopia.

It was that year Orson Welles' "War of the Worlds" aired on American radio creating panic across the nation. Americans were unaware it was occupants of the Earth who posed a much greater threat than aliens from space.

*   *   *

America was preparing for war and giving aid to Great Britain and France. Its direct involvement was yet to come.

Ignoring a non-aggression pact with the Soviet Union, Hitler sent his forces into the Soviet Union in June 1941.

Meantime, we heard little about a potential menace in the Orient, the expanding Japan empire that gave a new meaning to the "Land of the Rising Sun."

Blitzkrieg Begins

On September 1, 1939, Hitler's army invaded Poland. Within hours France and England declared war on Germany. World War II was underway.

In a lightning attack, German troops reinforced by tanks in what was called the Blitzkrieg swept through much of Western Europe. Nations tumbled like pins in a bowling lane.

*   *   *

As pre-teens, we had paid little attention to the war clouds our parents discussed. That changed on September 1, 1939. It was a Saturday and we were, as we always were, in Norman that night for the free outdoor movie store owner C. E. Cummings showed after his weekly auction.

The movie was forgotten in time. The conversation was not. For the first time I heard youngsters my age talk about war, knowing little about what it meant. One friend mentioned that the Polish people were having to dodge bombs, not knowing in his innocence that bombs could not be evaded like a ball on the playground.

We all had much to learn.

Older men we knew volunteered for the military forces long before President Roosevelt instituted the draft a year later. Workers who had been idled by the depression found jobs at the Burns City Naval Depot (now Crane) in nearby Martin County or a powder plant outside Charleston, more than an hour away.

On April 19, 1941, Cladie Bailey, commissioned eight years earlier after ROTC at Indiana University, was activated and ordered to report to Camp Livingston, Louisiana. He left school at Heltonville, where he taught mathematics and coached basketball, two weeks before the term ended. William Howard Thompson, another I.U. graduate from Heltonville, volunteered for the Army Air Corps and soon became a flight school instructor.

Other men we knew like Harold Lantz departed "when their numbers were up," the numbers being those assigned by what was called Selective Service System.

On September 29, 1941, The afternoon *Bedford Daily Times* reported 17 Lawrence County men were inducted that morning at Fort Harrison in Indianapolis, making a total of 135 drafted from the county to date.

That same day, the Associated Press revealed three British destroyers had been sunk by the Germans. It was obvious the Third Reich had control of the Atlantic.

Hitler's blitzkrieg, however, had begun its siege of Leningrad where Russians dug in for a long, bitter winter. Their resistance would prove that the German army at least could be stalled. Whether it could be beaten remained to be seen.

Prelude To War

Few omens on December 4, 1941, indicated what was ahead. Life for most folks around Heltonville continued as usual. Some men were away at military bases. Others had taken jobs at defense plants.

Little, on the surface was foreboding or ominous. The weather was too nice for complaints. It had been warm enough to cause apple trees to mistake Indian summer for spring; to bloom, then reach the apple-forming stage in a fatal welcome to a false spring.

Dale Norman, Herman Chambers, Bob Hillenberg, Opal Todd and the rest of the high school basketball team were in class on Thursday, a bit tired after a Wednesday night game at Smithville. No one razzed them about the 38-28 loss which the *Bedford Daily*

Times called "a rough and tough encounter." All games with Smithville were that way, and the loss by new coach Robert Barrett's team was not unexpected.

Grade school students looked forward to Saturday afternoon at the Lawrence Theater where they would see Tex Ritter in "Riding the Cherokee Trail" and Bela Lugosi in "Invisible Ghost." High school students made plans to see Edgar Bergen, Charlie McCarthy, Fibber McGee and Molly and a new actress named Lucille Ball in "Look Who's Laughing" at the Indiana. "Target for Tonight," a war movie whose promotions said was "actually filmed under fire," was showing at the VonRitz.

At grain elevators, wheat was bringing $1.07 a bushel, corn 60 cents, yellow soybeans $1.30, black soybeans $1.06. Hogs were being marketed at $9 to $10 a hundred weight, not a good price, but much better than the $2 of the recent depression years.

Food was plentiful. So were gasoline and tires. Stores offered shoes at bargain prices. Rationing was not yet a household word.

At the general stores, Maine potatoes were 29 cents for 10 pounds, Chippewas 29 cents for 15 pounds. Oranges sold for 19 cents a dozen, bananas 7 cents a pound. Butter was 35 cents a pound, roast pork 19 cents, bacon 25 cents.

Silk hose were advertised "$1 up" at Keller's store in Bedford, where "first quality" men's shirts were $1.49 and men's Oxfords were $2.98 "and up." Anyone who really wanted to spiffy up could buy spats for 69 cents.

Travel was unlimited. "Heltonville News" items in the *Daily Times* mentioned that Earl Todd had driven up from New Albany to visit his parents, Mr. and Mrs. Will Todd. Doyle Lantz, who had played on the basketball team a year earlier, had motored down from his new job at Anderson to spend the weekend with his folks, Mr. and Mrs. Jack Lantz.

The war abroad was barely mentioned, except for a short story headlined, "Nazis Battle Guerrillas in Serb Revolt." Two recruiters were in Bedford to interview young men interested in joining the Marines, but there was no mention of battles to come. Some men had volunteered for service, others had been drafted but most youths waited to see what developed in those uncertain days.

Their plans—and those of others in Heltonville and else-where across the nation—would change dramatically over that weekend to come.

The Associated Press reported on Friday, December 5, that Japan had sent President Roosevelt "what may be the fateful answer to the question of war or peace in the Pacific." If there was unease in Washington it was not a major concern for the average person in heartland America.

Pearl Harbor

SUNDAY, DECEMBER 7, 1941: A date that indeed lives in infamy. Japan launched a surprise attack on Pearl Harbor, the base called America's Gibraltar of the Pacific. It was morning in the Hawaiian Islands, mid-day in the eastern United States.

Early reports said at least 1,500 U.S. military personnel were killed and at least that many injured. Damage to ships and planes was extensive, the military officers in charge unaware of any pending disaster.

*   *   *

We had gone to church as usual that morning, then spent the afternoon up the road with our cousin Ray Hunter and some other friends. It was a clear, moderate day, warm enough to walk the hills. The problems of the world were far away and of little interest to us, or so we supposed.

Back home, I was surprised to find Mom and Dad near the battery-powered radio, there being little electric power in the area.

A few homes, however, did have electricity generated from their own small Delco systems that ran on kerosene engines. Some as I recall stored the electricity in a series of "wet cell" bat-teries.

(Neighbors, it was said, were in awe when they were invited to see lights burn and small engines run on the generated elec-tricity. Jake Cummings had one of the few electric generating systems in our area. We saved our dry cell radio batteries, Dad for Lowell Thomas and the news, Mom for "Mary Foster—The Editor's Daughter" and other soap operas, me and my siblings for shows like "Jack Armstrong—the all-American Boy" or "Little Orphan Annie.")

The mood was ominous. Neither parent smiled. They quietly related the news, explaining what happened, uncertain what would follow the attack on Hawaii. We did our chores that night and the next morning, expecting school to be a normal Monday.

It was not to be. Junior high and high school students met in our home room, which was the big assembly over the gymnasium. The bell to signal our departure to classrooms did not ring as usual. Instead Loren Raines, the principal, walked in, dressed as he often was in a light blue suit. His look was more somber than usual.

Raines was followed by Irvine East, the social studies teacher, who was carrying a big console radio.

The principal reviewed events of the previous day and said Congress would be in session that morning to hear a speech by President Franklin Roosevelt. East tuned in the radio, set inside a mahogany case, and asked the students at the back if they could hear.

There were no more than a total of 120 students in all six classes.

Students were subdued. A few older boys talked about enlisting in the Army or Navy. The younger ones just wished they could.

What whispering there was ended when President Roosevelt began:

"My fellow Americans."

The only interference was the radio's static and the hissing and clanking of the steam radiators on the wall.

"Yesterday, December 7, 1941 — a date which will live in infamy — the United States of America was suddenly and deliberately attacked by naval and air forces of the empire of Japan."

Seniors like Gene Dulin, Walter Owens and Lester Neff listened intently.

"The United States was at peace with that nation and, at the solicitation of Japan, was still in conversation with its government and its emperor looking toward the maintenance of peace in the Pacific . . ."

Junior Frank Hunter puts his chin in his hand and propped his elbow on the slanting desk top.

". . . The attack yesterday on the Hawaiian Islands has caused severe damage to American naval and military forces. Very many American lives were lost. In addition, American ships have been reported torpedoed on the high seas between San Francisco and Honolulu."

Sophomores like Bob Ford and Fred Lively looked at each other. No words were needed to express their feelings.

". . . Japan has, therefore, undertaken a surprise offensive extending throughout the Pacific area. The facts of yesterday speak for themselves. The people of the United States have already formed their opinions and well understand the implications of the very life and safety of the nation."

Freshman Earl Norman Jr., who would be the only boy to stay in that class and graduate in 1945, nodded knowingly.

". . . No matter how long it may take us to overcome this premeditated invasion, the American people in their righteous might will win through to absolute victory."

Donald Harrell and the other eighth graders were confident of that.

"I ask that the Congress declare that since the unprovoked and dastardly attack by Japan on Sunday, December 7, that a state of war has existed between the United States and the Japanese empire."

Leonard Chambers, Bob Bailey, Ralph Sherrill, Betty Blackwell, Irene Todd and the rest of the seventh graders joined in the applause that echoed through the assembly when the president finished.

A few minutes later the Senate voted 82-0 to declare war. Action followed in the House of Representatives, the outcome 388-1. Rep. Jeanette Rankin, R-Montana, was the only dissident, for whatever reasons we never knew.

We were sent to our classes, but every lesson plan, if teachers bothered to outline them, was discarded. Teachers tried—as best they could—to relate what war would mean. Neither they nor students grasped the extent of the burden ahead.

A few brave students predicted victory over "that podunk little island" within six weeks.

Roosevelt did not mention Germany in his short speech, but the U.S. would be at war with the Third Reich in a few days.

It was the first day of a war for Americans that was to last 1,345 days. All but the seventh and eighth graders would graduate before it was over. Some would die in the pursuit of victory.

For all it would be a morning they would never forget.

In time, the exodus of women from the home to the workplace began. They were like what the media called "Rosie the Riviter," working in defense plants and other factories, doing work that men had thought only they could do. It would, unknowingly at the time, change the fabric of America forever.

Sailors Weep

Dale "Herbie" Harrell, as a sailor aboard a destroyer, would tell us later how fate had distanced his ship from Pearl Harbor before the Japanese attack.

A week earlier, Harrell had been assigned to a captain's boat, a little gig with a crew of three that escorted officers from ship to shore or from shore to ship. The boat had plied the harbor, taking officers and their ladies to a dance aboard a battleship. Harrell watched the officers and the women board the ship.

In the parlance of his Southern Indiana home, the couples were "putting on the dog." Chances are he let his mind think of guitar and banjo music he was more accustomed to back in Heltonville, where he had grown up and graduated from high school.

Any threat of war seemed as remote as it had a year earlier when he had enlisted in the Navy in search of his future. He had seen envoys from Japan receive a royal welcome at Pearl Harbor on a stop from Tokyo to Washington. Any hint of animosity was lost in the pomp and ceremony.

A day or two after the dance, the Flusser left port as a screen for carriers sent on maneuvers around the Midway Islands.

Looking back, Harrell would think that "somebody from higher up must have told someone to order the carriers out to sea." It would prove to be a wise move.

Once the carriers were at sea near Midway, the destroyer was ordered to return to Pearl Harbor for patrol duty. In two more days, it would be within radio range of Honolulu and the sailors would be looking forward to a few hours of shore leave.

There would be no time for enjoyment on shore. The men on the destroyer learned on December 7, via the ship radio, that Pearl Harbor was under attack from Japanese planes.

Harrell recalled in the years to come the constant reminder via radio, "This is not a test. The Japanese are attacking Pearl Harbor... This is not a test. The Japanese are attacking Pearl Harbor." His ship was ordered to join up with other ships in the Pacific. They would not return to their base until about December 11.

It was then "Herbie" Harrell and his shipmates saw the havoc the enemy had caused. Harrell, a postal carrier later, never erased the scene from his mind. "There was not a dry eye on our ship. Seaman with tattoos and tales from a hundred ports wept," he said.

The Road Ahead

In the months ahead, the Japanese routed U.S. forces from the Philippines and continued their domination of the South Pacific. On his escape from the Philippines, Gen. Douglas MacArthur, in a testimonial to American determination, vowed, "I shall return."

Troops headed for action in Europe were diverted to Australia where they prepared for island warfare.

The "Manhattan Project," little known to most Americans, began in 1942. It would lead later to the demise of the Japanese Empire and become a weapon of mass destruction.

Slowly the tide turned. The U.S. won the battle of Midway on July 4, 1942, sinking four Japanese carriers. It was a victory that gave the allies superiority on the Pacific and boosted morale for all Americans.

In September, units of the 32nd Division landed in New Guinea and secured the island in combat with the Japanese. In November, allied forces landed in North Africa where they would eventually defeat the Germans and head for Southern Europe.

The invasion of Sicily that followed was a prelude to the invasion of the Italian mainland. On July 16, 1943, Roosevelt and Winston Churchill called on Italians to "live for civilization" rather than die for Hitler. On July 19, allies bombed Rome and six days later Mussolini, the Il Duce, was arrested and replaced by Marshal Pietro Bagdoglio, the Army Chief of Staff.

On September 8, the Italian surrender was announced as the U.S. Eighth Army landed in southern Italy. The Germans occupied Rome on September 10. Any hopes for a rapid liberation of Italy soon faded. After months of bitter fighting the American troops secured southern Italy, but it was not until April 1945 that the Germans surrendered northern Italy.

Mussolini was arrested again and jailed with his mistress, Clara Petacci. Both were lynched by Communist partisans who took them from their jail cells.

D-Day

The long-awaited invasion of France had come on June 6, 1944. In its third extra of the day, *The Indianapolis News* reported, "Allied forces landed in the Normandy area of France today and thrust several miles inland."

An estimated 4,000 ships and smaller crafts joined to escort American, Canadian and British to the invasion site. They were joined by 11,000 planes that strafed and bombed German installations prior to the landing of ground troops. That night President Roosevelt went on radio to ask the nation to pray for the Allied forces.

The strategy for the successful operation had been mapped by Gen. Dwight D. Eisenhower, the Supreme Commander of the Allied Expeditionary Force, and his staff.

Once again, hopes for a quick victory were premature. In what was to be called the Battle of the Bulge, the Germans went on the offensive, driving deep into allied positions. The news brought a chill to Christmas in American homes. It was devastating to relatives of men caught in the onslaught of the German Army in the midst of a European winter.

The tide changed on December 30, when Gen. George Patton sent 100,000 troops into a counter-offensive and drove the Germans back across the Luxembourg border into Germany.

After months of continual German setbacks, Hitler recognized his cause was lost. His body was found in a bunker at 3:30 p.m. April 30, 1945, ten days after his 56th birthday. At his side lay Eva Braun, said to be his mistress, although there were unconfirmed reports they may have wed days earlier. Hitler had shot himself, the revolver he used at his side. His Third Reich survived him . . . but for only a week. Eva Braun, had not used a second revolver, choosing poison to end her life.

As with all deaths of notorious individuals, rumors would continue for years. Some reports said Hitler had been spotted in Argentina, other said he had been captured by the Russians. As usual, the reports were wrong.

Germany Falls

On Monday, May 7, 1945, *The Indianapolis News* proclaimed in a giant headline "WAR ENDS IN EUROPE." The German aggression that started eight years earlier was over. The reign of terror Hitler expected to dominate the world had ended. Right had conquered evil.

Death Of Roosevelt

Franklin D. Roosevelt had not lived to see the demise of Hitler. The President whose leadership had led to victory died of cerebral hemorrhage on April 12, 1945, at Warm Springs, Georgia.

Harry Truman, a one-time farm boy, haberdasher and county commissioner had became President.

Meantime, the war in the Pacific continued. Gen. Douglas MacArthur had returned to Bataan as promised; U.S. forces were in the Philippines after routing the Japs (a term which later would be ridiculed as politically incorrect) from other islands they had captured.

Peace!

On August 6, 1945: *The Indianapolis News* headline read, "ATOMIC BOMB BLASTS JAPS! FORCE IS GREATEST EVER USED." The bold headline was appropriate for an event that momentous.

President Truman had authorized the use of the bomb in an effort to end the war. It was a move that is certain to have saved countless American lives if the Japanese homeland had to be invaded in the pursuit of victory.

The man whose credentials were doubted when he succeeded President Roosevelt had proved he too could make the decisions leadership required.

A second bomb followed later on Nagasaki. The devastation those bombs created when nuclear energy was released were a result of the "Manhattan Project" started in 1942.

The Aftermath

I was at Tipton in northern Indiana with 30 or so other Lawrence County teens — "Victory Farm Volunteers" we were called — when the first A-bomb fell. We detassled corn for Pioneer Seed Corn Company by day, bunked in corn storage bins by night.

Our news of the bomb came when we read the *Tipton Tribune* that night. None of us had a clue what an atomic bomb was, had no idea of its magnitude or its devastation. It would be days later before we would see the destruction in pictures in newspapers and on "Time Marches On" news clips at theaters.

We were back home on August 14 when Radio Tokyo reported Japan had surrendered, unconditionally as the allies demanded. I recall no great celebration at home or in our neighborhood.

Men we had known had died in battle and remained in graves overseas, a teen not much older than us had been lost at sea. Our older brother George had been killed in a car accident while stationed at an Air Corps base near Salinas, California.

Civilians as well as soldiers, sailors, marines, airmen and others in the military had helped make victory possible. Americans at home accepted rationing, contributed to bond drives, volunteered for duty as air wardens to detect any enemy planes and joined in "black outs" to keep Axis pilots from spotting any ground targets.

(We were walking home from a basketball game one night when a teen among us lighted a cigarette. "You moron," we yelled in jest, "that tip of fire can be seen by a Japanese pilot." He bragged he wasn't afraid and ignored our comment until, by coincidence, the sound of an airplane droned in the distance. He stamped out the butt of his Marvel cigarette on the Ind. 58 asphalt, dived into a ditch, clutched his hands over his head and swore to never again smoke at night. I don't think he ever earned a diploma, which was a testimonial to educators at Heltonville.)

Peace, it seemed, was an awakening after a long nightmare, the reality difficult to comprehend, the future brighter but still uncertain. The nation had been at war for so long, most adults reacted slowly even though the nation had prepared for demobilization and was ready to help veterans adjust to life back home.

They had seen the world, outgrown small towns and limited-acreage farms. Blacks, who had fought as valiantly as whites, no longer accepted minority status. They had earned the right to the assurances of the constitution. Women who had built the arsenals of war had learned independence from the confinement of home.

Government benefits helped veterans readjust to civilian life. Some joined what they called the "52-20 Club," which allowed them to receive $20 a week for 52 weeks, although most took jobs as soon as they found work. Many attended colleges under a GI Bill, millions married and bought homes with government loans.

*   *   *

A total of 405,399 Americans lost their lives during World War II, including 78,976 who remained missing in action. More than one-half the victims were returned to the United States for reinterment.

Thanks to those who gave their lives and others who fought the Axis empire, the world was at peace for the first time in the decade. Within five years Americans would be at war again, this time fighting the North Koreans in South Korea. A total of 54,246 American men and women would die in that engagement.

RATIONING

Within 10 days of Pearl Harbor the sale of new tires was prohibited and production of new cars would be limited to those who needed them for what already was being called "the war effort."

It was the first indication of the rationing ahead.

On April 28, President Roosevelt hinted his newest alphabet agency, the OPA (Office of Price Administration) might put a ceiling on prices to control prices and avoid gouging by opportunists and retailers.

A few months later he granted the OPA power to control wages, salaries and agricultural prices. Other events followed quickly:

April 27, 1942: All sugar sales stopped to be resumed a week later on May 4.

May 4: Americans lined up inside schoolhouses to register for their first books of rationing coupons, which allowed holders to resume buying sugar. The half-pound ration a week per person was said to be half of what the sugar-craving Americans normally bought. Makers of sweets were allotted slightly more than two-thirds of what they could have used.

The sugar shortage was not unexpected, much of it having been imported from the South Pacific where the war raged.

It was reported one-third of all food items were rationed at times. Ration books, issued by local boards, had red, green, brown and blue stamps. Each family member was issued a ration book and each stamp indicated both its monetary value and a number of points. Items of food required a set number of points, a can of food, for example might require 16 ration points.

Nº 641|526 DY

UNITED STATES OF AMERICA
OFFICE OF PRICE ADMINISTRATION

WAR RATION BOOK FOUR

Issued to _____ *Nelson E. Chambers*
(Print first, middle, and last names)

Complete address _____ *72 1 Monroe*

_____ *Evansville, Ind.*

READ BEFORE SIGNING

In accepting this book, I recognize that it remains the property of the United States Government. I will use it only in the manner and for the purposes authorized by the Office of Price Administration.

Void if Altered _____
(Signature)

It is a criminal offense to violate rationing regulations.
OPA Form R-145

16—25570-1

When a family exhausted its points for certain type foods, it could not buy more until the ration book's expiration date.

Additional points, however, could be earned by saving meat drippings, which was a part of a "save-fats" campaign.

May 14, 1942: Gas was rationed in 17 states in the eastern part of the country after U-boats (German submarines) began to sink supply ships as they attempted to cross the Atlantic. Limited sales were extended to all states that December.

Every car had a ration stamp pasted on its windshield, each identified by a letter, A stamps for travel deemed "non-essential;" B stamps for those whose work required travel; C stamps for doctors and emergency workers, and X designated for VIPs such as U.S. senators and representatives.

Even in war, politicians sometimes put themselves first, but the X stamp was discontinued after complaints by the American populace.

That spring, American housewives were asked to make a "vital" contribution to the war effort during spring housecleaning.

"Mrs. America" was told to "help feed factories the scrap they need by turning in old junk." The plea explained:

"Easements, attics, garages, closets all can yield vast hoardings of old rubber, scrap metal, rags, waste paper—scrap materials that can help provide vital war materiel. Metals will soon be going into guns, tanks, ships, shells. Old rubber will become tank treads, gas masks, lifeboat rafts, pontoon bridges."

Most rationing would continue to war's end and it would be 1947 before sugar again would be plentiful.

Making Do

As did most farm families, ours endured rationing easier than those in cities and towns. Like other families across the nation our sacrifices were microscopic to those faced by the Americans who defended us.

Mom never complained about food rationing, but it was not easy for Dad to adjust to limited sugar. He had been known to sprinkle sugar on sugar. He coated oatmeal with a sugar topping, sweetened already sweet apple pie and drank coffee made up of equal parts of cream, coffee and sugar.

He found Karo syrup and a few other experiments were no substitute.

Other than that we all fared well. Families in town raised a few vegetables in small "Victory Gardens." We had one that covered almost an acre and every inch it seemed was used to produce corn, tomatoes, potatoes and yams, green beans, radishes and onions.

Once the growing season ended, the cellar was lined with enough canned goods to feed an Army battalion.

Our milk came from the cows we kept, our butter churned from cream separated from the milk. Eggs were fresh from the nests in the hen house and meat came from the hogs we butchered at home.

Farms were allotted extra gasoline for tractors and the rationed amount met our needs for the Farmall H.

Synthetic Tires

Tires for cars and trucks posed a vexing and continual problem. Individuals soon learned the new synthetic types blew out after minimum usage.

After a study the Indiana State Police reported in 1943 officers had tested 158 of the new synthetic tires and found two-thirds of them had to be replaced before they were driven 1,500 miles. The reason for blowouts came, the study showed, when "blisters formed when heat was generated at even the slightest excess speed."

Excess speed in those war years was anything over 35 mph.

Dad didn't need a state police test to know that. He already knew the tires exploded at speeds under 35. Dad didn't know the meaning of pretense. He made no effort to hide any displeasure that came his way and synthetic tires brought him a lot of consternation.

He accepted rationing, used sweetener in his coffee instead of sugar, and, to save gasoline, made only trips that were really necessary.

But that didn't keep him from erupting when one of the new synthetic tires for which he had paid a premium price blew itself to smithereens. He knew the government had turned to synthetic tire production because ninety-seven percent of the rubber used in the United States came from South Pacific islands occupied by the Japanese.

Most government claims that synthetics were better than natural rubber in many respects came from bureaucrats and rubber company officials, not from drivers who depended on them.

The synthetic tires looked as good as those made from rubber. The tread was thick, but like beauty it was only skin deep. Dad soon learned that. He made a couple of short trips on the tires before driving to Bedford for a mowing machine part. En route home he heard a "clap, clap, clap," then a loud "boom." One of the new tires had blown.

A few days later, we were headed to Brownstown, the temperature in the 90s, hot enough to fry an egg on the concrete pavement of U.S. 50. A second synthetic tire blew. It too was replaced with a well-worn tire of pre-war vintage, but only after Dad lamented: "Buying them damned fake tires is worse than putting money in a shell game at a county fair."

When we mentioned that the tires were supposed to be replaced free after blowouts, Dad railed, "That's like getting a bad check to replace one that has already bounced."

He had no choice, though, but to buy more synthetic tires. Each time he heard a "clap, clap, clap," he just pulled over to the side of the road, changed the tire and continued to develop his vocabulary. As long as America was at war. it was the least he could do.

The War Effort

It was a time of patriotism, a time when Americans had faith in their government and trust in their leaders. It was a time of a war in which there were few dissenters.

Everyone had a role, be it as a participant, a defense worker, a civil defense volunteer, a food producer or a fund raiser.

Students throughout the nation were too young to serve, not old enough to work in war plants. They became fund raisers, instead. And in doing so, they learned the virtues of thrift, the yields that result from investments, and the satisfaction that came from being a part of something bigger than themselves.

We eighth graders spent the time allotted for physical education to removing debris from the site of the school fire. The scrap iron brought some money for the school and helped the war effort.

War Bonds

Most of us had little money. Until the U.S. entered the war against Japan and Germany, we spent any dime we had for nickel Nehi Sodas and five-cent candy bars. Once the war started it did not seem patriotic to gratify our desires for treats when some of our teachers and older brothers were at war.

We could not, had we chosen, escape the needs for our help. Newspapers reminded us each week. Full page ads called the enemy "Japs," a term that would be labeled "politically incorrect" 50 years later. Those advertisements carried headlines such as, "The job in the Pacific is not finished!"

The text showed a G.I. in a foxhole saying, "There are still millions of tough, brutal Japs to lick. Every Jap we kill makes my chances of getting home better, and it costs plenty to kill a Jap." The ads, which disclosed that a B-29 bomber cost $600,000 and an M-4 tank $67,417, concluded with another reminder:

"Just as long as a single Japanese aims a gun at our men, we must continue to buy War Bonds." None of us could hope to save enough to buy a war bond outright. But each dime we had would buy a 10-cent saving stamp. If we earned extra money it could buy 25-cent, 50-cent, $1 or $5 stamps, which could be placed in a book that eventually could be converted to a war bond worth $25 at maturity. Each stamp helped fund the war, as did each pound of tin or bit of scrap iron we salvaged.

Each campaign resulted in increased sales of stamps and bonds. Each student was proud when Principal Raines read the results of one War Bond drive. We had bought an even $1,000 in stamps and bonds. Our parents, who had lived throughout Pleasant Run Township, had invested another $14,666.

If any of the donors had depleted the accounts they had saved for Christmas presents, so be it. The best gift would be in knowing, in a few years, not a single Japanese soldier would be aiming a gun at an American.

Milkweed and Kapok

Radio shows like "Jack Armstrong," became less important. They seemed secondary to chores and the constant reminders of "the war effort." Our parents were surprised, but certainly not disappointed that we no longer griped when there was work to be done.

We were not alone. No matter how old or how young, each American it seemed, was involved in helping the armed forces win their battles with the Germans in Europe, the Japanese in the Pacific. All would endure breakfast cereal without sugar, wear worn shoes, walk home from school after basketball and travel only when auto trips were absolutely necessary.

Instead of radio shows, we would traipse on some afternoon to ditches and swamps, feed sacks in hand, oblivious to weeds and briars, in search of milkweed pods. Each pod gathered would be added to those found by other students at school, so we continued our search while our chores awaited.

And the Heltonville collection would become a part of the entire Lawrence County output. We were told milkweed could, indirectly, help win the war because the pods contained kapok, a silky fiber suitable for insulation and padding in life preservers. Ten pounds of pods were said to be enough for one life jacket.

Each of us proudly toted sacks to school to be added to the pile of bags in a hallway. We expected no recognition for patriotism exceeded personal gratification.

It was later we learned what we had accomplished. O. O. Hall, the Lawrence County school superintendent, announced that students in the county had collected 500 bags, 2,500 pounds, of milkweed pods.

"Our students are responsible for 250 more preservers," Hall said. Needmore students had turned in 101 bags, twice as many as those at Heltonville. The two schools were rivals in sports, but this had been a competition in which there were no losers. All had joined in "the War Effort."

We went back to "Jack Armstrong" for a few days. Within another week it would be time for us to engage in other war efforts.

Goody Few Shoes

Without any advance warning, James Byrne, the Economic stabilization director, said on February 8, 1943, that each American would be limited to three pairs of shoes per year. "He had issued the decree," Miss Clark, a teacher, read from the paper, "to make certain that the American people will continue to have all the shoes they need."

The War Production Board had estimated shoe leather and reclaimed rubber would be available for only 335,000,000 pairs of civilian footwear. That was 105,000,000 fewer pairs than were made in 1942, Miss Clark explained, condensing the information as she read.

Miss Clark was not as fashion conscious as some of the teachers, but she cared about her appearance and always made sure her shoes looked new.

The freshmen girls were at an age when they wanted to appear older so the junior and senior boys would pay attention to them. They were just beginning to look ahead to the days when they could wear high heels. Miss Clark often used the news of the day to encourage discussion and to help students see how it related to them.

It was obvious from the response that the girls were more concerned than the boys about shoes. Some of them groaned when Miss Clark read that gold and silver and any two-tone shoes were out for the duration. Colors would be limited to white, black, town brown and Army russet.

And some of them also sighed when she continued: "Women's shoe heels are to be limited to not more than 2½ inches and platforms... those extra thick soles some women fancy... are forbidden."

A few girls didn't relate at all. They were from big families who couldn't afford three pairs of shoes each year for each child, regardless of the style.

As usual, Gordy was the first to speak. "I don't get but one pair of shoes a year. And that's right before school starts."

The other boys unconsciously looked toward their feet. Gordy had worn the same pair since Labor Day. The sole on one was fastened to the toe with a thin wire twisted at the side.

He wasn't alone. Farm boys' shoes were essentials, not luxuries. Like Gordy, only a few had more than one pair, except maybe for overshoes, at one time.

Miss Clark, aware she was supposed to be teaching English, cut off the conversation about that time. But the subject came up again the next morning.

Gordy said, "I mentioned shoe-rationing to my folks last night that we each would be limited to three pair a year. Mom laughed and told Dad, 'Looks like you're going to have to go to the bank and borrow enough money for us to buy two more pair than usual for each of the kids.' "

I told Miss Clark and the girls that my dad wanted them to know he'd trade stamps, one for shoe rationing for one for a pound of sugar.

As with food and gasoline, those who complained about shoes learned to live with their allotments. In the summer when we walked barefoot on gravel roads we knew we were helping the war effort by saving shoe leather.

Lucky Strike Green

LS/MFT on the package meant "Lucky Strike means fine tobacco."

It also meant its maker contributed to the war effort.

Lucky Strikes were among cigarettes like Marvels, Old Gold, Philip Morris, Kools, Camels, Chesterfields and Wings, which remained plentiful in WWII. For those who could roll their own, bags of Bull Durham were available.

It would be two decades later before the surgeon general of the nation would declare tobacco was harmful to health.

Each brand of cigarettes had its own attractive package, Lucky Strike's green cover being one that stood out. The war changed that. The area around the red bullseye on the package was no longer green. It was white.

Advertisements suddenly boasted, "Lucky Strike green has gone to war. The materials used to make the green color, we were told, were needed for the war effort.

There were no chemistry classes at Heltonville, but a teacher explained the green coloring used in ink contained chromium, which the dictionary said was a lustrous, hard, steel-gray metallic element, resistant to tarnish and corrosion." It could harden steel alloys.

Those characteristics made Lucky Strike green useful in paint for tanks and other weapons and war materiels.

Lucky Strike had indeed gone to war. And so had millions of young men and women.

TRANSPORTATION

Aviation was still in its infancy at the start of the 1930s even though air travel was becoming more popular.

Knute Rockne, the famed Notre Dame football coach, was among eight passengers killed when a tri-engine Fokker crashed into a pasture in Kansas on March 31, 1931.

On March 1, 1932 newspapers headlined the kidnapping of Charles Augustus Lindbergh Jr.

The young son of the man who made flight familiar was taken from his parents' home at Hopewell, New Jersey, by a kidnapper who climbed a ladder to a second-story nursery.

A hand-scrawled note demanded a ransom the news media claimed was $50,000.

It was the senior Lindbergh, dubbed "The Lone Eagle," who had become an international idol on May 23, 1927, when he made the first solo flight across the Atlantic. It was a 3,800-mile journey in the tiny single-engine plane called the "Spirit of St. Louis."

On that night five years later, he again was alone, searching in the darkness of his estate for the son who had meant more to him than the accolades he continued to receive.

The decomposed body of Lindbergh's son was discovered by truck driver William Allen about two miles from the Lindbergh home on May 12, 1932.

Examiners said the cause of death was a fractured skull.

Bruno Richard Hauptman, an illegal German immigrant, was arrested on September 19, 1934. He had a ransom bill with him; another $14,000 of the money was found in his garage.

Hauptmann denied any involvement. He was convicted in a trial conducted in a circus-like atmosphere and executed April 3, 1936, in Trenton, New Jersey. It would be the first in a series of so-called "trials of the century" that would end with O.J. Simpson's acquittal for the murder of his estranged wife.

*   *   *

Eight decades later, the Hauptmann trial is a faint memory of conversations among my parents and their friends. We recall some expression of doubts about Hauptmann's guilt, there being skeptics then as there would continue to be about most events that create extensive media coverage.

Death From Above

The Lindbergh flight across the Atlantic was before we were born. In our rural isolation, we saw few airplanes and each one we saw was a major event for a youngster in bib overalls. We heard the sound of the engines, spotted the planes on a distant horizon and watched in fascination as the air machines seemed to float across the unpolluted skies to a destination unknown to us.

Will Rogers, the cowboy philosopher actor, and pilot, Wiley Post, who had circled the earth in a plane, died on August 14, 1935, when their plane crashed in a fog over Point Barrow, Alaska.

Air travel increased in the 1930s and the first commercial flight crossed the Atlantic in 1939. It was the year the helicopter was invented.

Actress Carol Lombard, wife of actor Clark Gable, was among 22 passengers who died when a TWA plane crashed into Table Rock Mountain on the eastern slope of Death Valley. She was en route home from Indianapolis where she had promoted the sale of U.S. defense bonds.

We would continue to observe the flights, which became frequent in World War II when the Army Air Corps trained pilots to fly P-26 planes based at Freeman Field at nearby Seymour. The more adventurous among us daydreamed we were at the controls, gliding over the wooded hills and open fields we now could only see at ground level.

We would learn later that bravery is directly proportional to the distance from the battle.

The Hindenburg

On May 7, 1937, newspaper headlines bannered the disaster, "Hindenburg Burns On Descent, At Least 35 Dead."

The Hindenburg, the pride of Adolph Hitler's Third Reich, had made the flight across the Atlantic from Germany. A luxurious flying hotel, it was 800 feet long and faster than any ship at sea. It was a prologue, some said, to safe travel of the future.

It was not to be. As it prepared to land at the Lakehurst, New Jersey, Naval Station it burst into flames. Within seconds, the largest airship ever built turned into a ball of fire. Still and motion pictures caught the drama for the nation to see again and again over the years to come.

Speculation about the cause began immediately. Some considered it sabotage by those opposed to the Nazis who held power in Germany.

In the end it was determined the Germans had designed what some called "a flying bomb waiting to explode." The outer skin, once ignited, was to burn, it was said, "like dry leaves."

(That disaster was a lesson for news reporters. One man assigned to cover the arrival of the Hindenburg told other newsmen it would be just a routine event and left the area to watch a movie.)

(Years later on Halloween Night, 1963, a critic covering an ice show at the Coliseum on the Indiana State Fairgrounds, departed early, telling a reporter nearby, "If anything exciting happens after I leave, just tack it onto the end of my story." A few minutes later an explosion beneath a grandstand killed 67 people and wounded 224 more.)

*   *   *

We do not recall seeing any dirigibles up to that time the Hindenburg burned. They were not alien, however, to Elmer Harrell, an older neighbor and friend.

Elmer had attended the one-room grade school at Zelma, where he and other elementary students learned the basics from teacher Eva Henderson. He remembered strange noises from out of the clouds, when planes began to soar across the sky. "It was an automatic recess when an airplane went over. We all went outside to watch as long as we could see it."

He recalled the time a blimp had passed. "That turned out to be an hour recess. It floated slowly from the north to the south and we watched it drift out of sight." It was an event that remained clear into the twilight of his life.

Earhart Disappears

A news dispatch on July 5, 1937 reported: "United States battleships, destroyers and airplanes—mobilized in one of the greatest sea hunts of all time—raced over the South Pacific today where Amelia Earhart and Frederick Noonan are believed floating in a land plane so badly waterlogged that it can't last much longer."

The United Press said amateur radio operators in Hawaii had heard Earhart's plea for help and the words, "Still alive. Better hurry. Tell husband all right."

The noted aviatrix, a pioneer among women pilots, was attempting to circle the globe. Neither she nor Noonan were ever found.

Speculation about their fate continued into the 21st Century. Rumors ranged from "captured by the Japanese" to "lost at sea." No proof of what really occurred has ever been determined.

It was a mystery that is still debated.

Small Planes

Three incidents that involved small airplanes have remained clear over the decades.

* Mid-1940s: A doctor, whose name is lost in time, came from out of the sky to treat a family member who needed medical care at our home.

A pilot who owned his own plane, the doctor didn't need a landing strip. He spotted a stubble field on a flat stretch of land, made a smooth landing and taxied within a few feet of a barbed wire fence a hop, skip and jump from the house.

He made a quick transition from pilot to doctor, walked quickly, medical bag in hand, to the house, cared for the patient, left some medication and returned to the plane.

He waved before his take off, which was as smooth as the landing. He would later tell my dad the house call via the plane was a welcome diversion from seeing patients in his office.

*   *   *

* JULY, 1946: He was no Waldo Pepper, this pilot who brought instant excitement to Zelma on that warm afternoon one July Sunday in 1946.

But he was the best pilot the youngsters—and some of the adults—had ever seen.

He had landed his Aeronica Chief down in the wheat stubble on the Fountain farm and taxied up alongside Ind. 58 across from Fred Evans' house, stopping a hundred yards or so from the Milwaukee Railroad.

By the time he unstrapped himself, opened the cockpit door and hopped down, half the people within a mile of the place were either there or on their way.

"Name's Bill," he said, smiling and waving like he was Lindbergh and had just crossed the Atlantic.

Bill was Bill Beaman, who was or later would be a writer for the *Bedford Times-Mail*. He announced, "I'll give anyone here a chance to fly 15-minutes with me for $1.50. Any takers?"

Before anyone could take up his offer, the comments came. Bill said later he'd heard them all before.

"If God had wanted me to fly, he'd have given me wings," a farmer down the road said.

I was at the curious age, 14 or 15, and eager for the attention. I handed Bill a wilted $1 bill and 50 cents in change. Bill boosted me into the cockpit, made sure my harness was fastened and taxied down the makeshift runway, revving the single engine to a steady whine. The Aeronica bounded along the stubble as it neared a drainage ditch.

Bill pulled back the control wheel and the plane lifted easily skyward, much slower than speed of my heart. Once he leveled out, he flew over our farm, banking so I could get a good view of the house and barn. We took a look over Mundell Church, followed the railroad tracks to Norman and returned to the field where the plane landed as smoothly as a feather.

By then, a half dozen others were in line for the experience. Bill took each of them for their solo flights. When I thought he had made his last trip, he motioned for me.

"I owe you a favor for showing those other folks it was safe to fly. Want to go for another trip?" It was like asking if I wanted a Three Musketeers bar or a milkshake.

Airborne again, he asked, "Want to drive?"

"Yep," I replied. "Just show me what to do?" He made me think I had total control, although I didn't.

I talked about the rides continually for a day. My dad heard more about it than he cared to hear, but Mom just said, "Let the boy enjoy the thrill. He'll be back to earth in a day or two."

*   *   *

*A FALL SUNDAY, 1946: It was a day like no other day, a day when the jet age came to Heltonville. It came from out of the sky as a Shooting Star, a P-80 Lockheed jet, skidded to a stop on Floyd Johnson's place out where Groundhog Road joined Powerline Road.

It was a big event for youngsters around town who had watched those propeller driven PT-26s from Freeman Field. This was a jet, which we had never seen.

The war had ended a year earlier and military planes had all but disappeared from the skies over the bucolic terrain. But we teens still looked to the skies at the roar of engines.

We were in Heltonville that afternoon, in search of entertainment, when a motorist shouted a plane was down. We quickly found a ride to the farm two miles away, where a curious crowd had gathered.

The plane, already off-limits to civilians, was a few hundred feet from the farm house. Except for some damage to the bottom of the fuselage, it looked none the worse for the experience.

"That means the flame went out and there was nothing to power the jet-propulsion engine, which happens to be an Allison J33-A-9. Made in Indianapolis," explained classmate Donald Todd.

For a 16-year-old farm kid, it was an astute observation.

A smart aleck in the crowd announced the pilot was safe. "He's somewhere changing his pants," he said, laughing at his remark.

In a few hours, the plane was removed from the scene and life returned to normal. The incident would remain vivid for a lifetime.

Modern aviation was in its infancy but we did not know how quickly it would advance or dare dream of space travel or flights to the moon.

Railroads

We entered life when railroads had reached a gradual descent from their zenith. Trains were discontinuing stops in small towns, many no longer carried passengers and the frequency of runs widened.

Farmers who once shipped products by train had turned to men who picked up cream, eggs and other produce, then delivered them to markets.

We were most familiar with the Milwaukee Road, which ran a mile north of our farm. At its peak it had linked 38 towns along a 147.9-mile route across southern Indiana from Terre Haute to Westport.

My dad recalled shipping products from a small depot in Zelma and riding trains to Bedford occasionally, but that stop had been eliminated before I was old enough to remember.

The trains continued to stop in Heltonville, where a side rail allowed cars to be loaded with freight. And a spur line led to the mill east of town where flatcars were loaded with finished stone that would be taken to New York and Washington to become part of the nation's most impressive edifices.

I did not learn until I was an adult that my grandfather, George Cummings, had been killed at a crossing on the railroad. He was en route into Heltonville in a horse-drawn wagon to pick up a casket for a neighbor who had died of typhoid. It was a month before my mother's sixth birthday.

My first experience with interstate commerce came via the railroad during a drought in the northeast. Dairy farms in northern New York, desperate for feed for their cows, called on the Midwest for hay. We hauled enough loads to fill a boxcar at the Heltonville depot, stacking a few hundred bales into the confined space.

A few other farmers jested that my dad would never see a penny for the hay or for our efforts to load it. Dad shrugged and said, as if he had been a professor in economics, "Business is based on trust. If you get an order to deliver somethin' you trust the buyer to pay for it."

He did get a bit antsy, however, before the check arrived.

I do not recall too many incidents involving the Milwaukee Road except contests to see which of us could walk the rails the farthest without falling off.

I also watched hobos of the depression wave from the box cars. A few of them hopped off from time to time to seek handouts of food when the trains slowed. Oh, we soaped the tracks as most kids did, then watched the locomotives spin their wheels as they ascended toward the stone mill. If we had an extra penny, which was seldom, we laid it on the tracks for the train to flatten. When a child, one does childish things.

The depot at Heltonville closed a few years later and the station relocated for use as a home. In the years ahead the rails would be uprooted and trains left as a part of the area's lore. With them went Cale, Coxton, Shawswick Station and other places that have all but disappeared. Only hints of the rail bed remain as evidence of the road's importance.

Some other 14 year olds fibbed about their ages and worked for the railroad one summer, but Dad said we had tomato fields to plant and fields to work at home.

An old timetable of the Milwaukee's route remains a treasure. Trains left the Hulman Station in Terre Haute at 4:21 a.m., arrived in Heltonville at 7:33 a.m. and reached Wesport at 11:51 a.m. It returned to Terre Haute at 6:35 p.m.

Once passenger service was discontinued, a small motor bus ran on Ind. 58 between Seymour and Bedford for a few years. The number of riders declined and it was discontinued around 1950.

Two other railroads, the Monon and the Baltimore and Ohio, served our area. The Monon at its peak had 600 miles of lines in Indiana and linked Louisville, Indianapolis and Chicago with dozens of other towns.

The B & O ran from Huron through Mitchell, Tunnelton and Fort Ritner in southern Lawrence County. I did not board a passenger train until the early 1950s when I returned to an Army base at Baltimore.

Automobiles

Our parents (like most women of her time, my mom never learned to drive) had a Whippet, I was told, when I was an infant. It had replaced an Overland, both of which were made by the Willy-Overland Company. The Whippet, it was said, was named for the Whippet, a dog that was small but swift.

Speed was not an asset for cars in the early 1930s. The roads were narrow, winding, mostly unpaved, railroad crossings unmarked. Wrecks were numerous, many drivers unqualified.

Our neighbor Ben Kindred drove a Model T then, as he would into the 1940s, reluctant to attempt to shift gears which was required in later models. Ben and his wife, Ellie, had no children and seldom left home, except to attend church. That stopped abruptly—because of the Model T—one Sunday.

Ben parked the Ford in the church lot, backing it into a spot to make sure he had room to crank it to a start later. Ellie walked up the steps and joined the women inside. Ben waited outside for the bell to ring, talking with other farmers about crops and the weather.

After the services, Ellie remained inside to talk. Ben visited with the men a few minutes and then began to shuffle from one foot to the other. His neighbors knew he was getting perturbed when he pulled out each suspender and let it pop back against his perspiration-darkened shirt.

It was obvious he was ready to head home and that Ellie's dallying was to blame for his impatience. His face had turned red by the time Ellie walked down the steps. He followed her to the car, then set the spark and the gas levers and fidgeted with some other instruments as she eased into the back seat where she always sat.

Ben walked to the front of the car, grabbed the crank and gave it a twist. Then another. The car lurched forward. Ben jumped to the side to avoid being hit. The car crossed Powerline (now Mundell Church) Road, which ran beside the church, banged against the clay bank and stopped, still chugging as only a Model-T could.

Ellie looked scared.

Ben ran as fast as his aging legs would take him to the car, jumped in and shifted into reverse. He backed out quickly, his bronze face an even darker red.

He didn't make his getaway fast enough to keep onlookers from hearing Ellie vent her embarrassment. They returned to church only for a few funerals. The minister was never brave enough to visit them to seek their return.

Modern Necessities

A decline in new car sales in the depression did not indicate the nation had forsaken the auto as a means of transportation. By then, cars had become a necessity. Most owners drove their cars for longer periods or traded for less used models.

Cheaper cars meant a decline in the sale of Dusenberg, Pierce Arrow and Stutz and other luxury cars whose makers refused to reduce quality in order to appeal to average Americans. As those expensive models faded from show rooms, cars became less important as status symbols that separated the rich and the poor.

Styling remained important, however. More functional cars produced in the late 1930s without chrome looked out-of-date and failed to sell well. Despite a poor economy, motorists chose originality and design over price.

Most cars before World War II were without turn signals, automatic transmissions, air-conditioning, power steering, temperature controls and other innovations. Lights were illuminated by a switch on the dash and dimmed by a switch on the floor board. The ignition came from a key inserted on the dashboard. Engines were still simple, computers were years away and many owners could make their own repairs.

Cars, though, had become more streamline in design—and more affordable—in the 1930s. A new Studebaker Champion was advertised late in the decade for as low as $795. Almost every county seat had General Motors, Ford, Chrysler and other dealers eager to attract buyers.

Money remained scarce, however, until nearby defense plants opened. Some workers we knew helped pay for the cheaper cars when they charged co-workers for rides to places like Crane and Charlestown.

Civilian auto production stopped once World War II started and factories turned to the needs of the military forces. Roadside mechanics like Abe Martin in Heltonville made engine repairs and kept cars and trucks running. Others like Cecil Cummings rebuilt wrecks and did other body work.

Meantime, Detroit automakers shifted from cars to vehicles of war. Mass production on assembly lines pioneered by the Ford Motor Company increased weapons production and gave corporate consumerism a new image.

Auto designers assigned to defense work, observed the sleekness of military airplanes like the P-38. They would later use similar styling on cars, one of those designs, according to some reports, the tailfins of the 1950s.

Buick A Favorite

My dad traded used cars often in the 1930s, owning an Overland, a Studebaker, a Chevrolet or two and finally a Buick. I was with him in 1940 when he traded the Chevy and $375 for a three-year-old Buick, which would forever, despite buying other cars later, remain his favorite.

We drove that Buick through World War II and beyond before he sold it for $600. His profit would be his loss for he never again found a car he liked as well.

And my brother and I never stopped razzing him about an incident that arose from the car's sale.

Dad never looked in the mirror, except to shave or comb his hair which remained jet black almost until he died at 95. He was not a person who navigated by the star of self-interest.

The only things false about him were his teeth. And he wore them begrudgingly, to please Mom. When she was not with him, he took out the teeth and placed them in the glove compartment the Buick. The charade went on for months, a secret that the sale of the car revealed.

Dad turned over the keys to buyer Horace George, a storekeeper in Norman, pocketed the check and returned home. Cars were still hard to find in that post-war year, so Dad bought a 1934 Chevrolet to use in the interim.

It wasn't until Sunday morning when Mom noticed his sunken cheeks. "If you want to be seen with me, you'd better put in your teeth," she said.

"Can't find them," Dad replied. "And I don't remember where I put them." Mom stomped into church without waiting for him. In the midst of the sermon he realized his "choppers" might be in the Buick.

Meantime, Horace had resold the car. Dad tracked down the buyer, recovered his teeth and told the buyer, "Reckon you don't mind if I take these."

The man nodded. "Guess you've missed them?"

Dad patted a fender of the Buick and said, "Not as much as I miss the car."

Kindly Repairman

It was Cecil Cummings who came to our aid after my first wreck, a collision with an unlighted and disabled truck that had stopped on a curve in U.S. 50 at the east entrance to Bedford.

The truck driver had no insurance, but, after some urging by the Lawrence County sheriff, agreed to provide $50 for the repair of our car. Cecil fixed it as good as new, replacing a fender and doing extensive repairs. I expected the worse when he gave Dad the bill at the shop in Heltonville.

He looked it over and said, "This is going to cost you money, son. An entire dime."

Cecil had, somehow, magically, done the repairs for $50.10. I could not avoid a small smile when I remembered that bill 25 years later at calling hours for Cecil at the Jones Funeral Home in Heltonville before his funeral.

Cars became more complicated, mechanics were required to be technicians and roadside repair shops disappeared.

*   *   *

Cars and vans remain works in progress. Improvements continue, new safety requirements are demanded and few families can seem to exist with less than two vehicles and homes with four-car garages are not uncommon.

Roads

Gone, too, are the road signs of that area. "Tractors With Lugs Prohibited," proclaimed signs on Ind. 58, a warning to farmers whose machines did not yet run on rubber. Burma Shave signs used humor to offer somber advice for motorists. "Cabins $3 and Up" promoted roadside lodging on U.S. 50 and other interstate routes. Mail Pouch tobacco signs and See Rock City signs stood out on barns otherwise vacant of color. A simple "Eats" was enough to attract diners to mom and pop restaurants long before McDonald's sold hamburgers by the millions.

Except for "The War," gas was cheap and plentiful, five gallons, $1, with a choice of a crystal or china item thrown in.

Attendants at service stations operated the pumps, cleaned windshields, checked oil gauges, gave directions and made change from coin dispensers at belt level.

Cars, then as now, were frequent targets of theft. My older brother's 1937 Ford was stolen one Saturday night while we attended a movie in Bedford. We took a taxi back home, a ten mile trip that cost $6 which seemed like the national debt to us.

Roads were two-lane and ran through the hearts of towns, not around them. Drivers and passengers had a sense of what each city was like. Those who could afford the price stayed in what seemed like elegant hotels like the Greystone in Bedford, whose demise would come with the advent of motels.

Roads crossed railroad tracks not on bridges that passed over them. "Narrow Bridge" signs were not needed for all bridges were narrow. Except in mountains or ranges of hills, roads followed elevations and seldom sliced through them. Many routes followed paths of least resistance.

Danger appeared to loom each mile. Three teens we knew from Heltonville were killed one Sunday afternoon as they walked to a ball diamond near our home on Ind. 58. They were hit on the upside of a hill as two cars approached from opposite directions.

A narrow overhead railroad trestle in the center of two 90-degree turns posed a constant hazard. It allowed room for but one car and drivers would use their horns to alert on-coming motorists. Caution was required.

Brother Wayne tooted the car's horn one afternoon, heard no response and proceeded slowly through the underpass. His car and one that approached downhill onto the turn collided.

Wayne was blameless but not in the mind of the other driver. He looked at Wayne and said, "This would not have happened if you hed been through here two minutes ago."

Huh? Wayne laughed. But the man was serious, adding, "Everybody knows I come through here from work at the exact same time every day. You should have known that."

He finally agreed to pay the damage to his own car. But he did remind Wayne, "Don't you ever come through that trestle again when I'm on the way home."

CRIME

The Dillinger Gang

Crime did not take a holiday during the depression. It became again a growth industry.

News headlines on January 26, 1934, reported the capture of John Dillinger, the Hoosier-born gangster, and his men at Tucson, Arizona.

In the midst of the Great Depression, Dillinger had become a hero of sorts to some Hoosiers who had lost their savings when banks failed. The Dillinger gang had turned bank robbery into a business, and some people admitted, reluctantly, a vicarious satisfaction at the news of each holdup.

Back in his hometown of Mooresville, some residents claimed the farm youth's career went from bad to worse when he was sentenced to the State Reformatory at Pendleton after an armed robbery of a town grocer in 1924. Expecting a more lenient sentence, Dillinger, without the advice of an attorney, pleaded guilty.

"Ten to twenty years," the judge ruled, leaving Dillinger bitter, resentful and in a mood for revenge. The fact an accomplice got a much shorter term added to his anger.

Less than a month later, Dillinger, age 18, made his first attempt to escape. It would not be his last.

It was at the reformatory, he met Harry Pierpont and Homer Van Meter, both of whom would add to their criminal resumes. All eventually would be transferred to the State Prison at Michigan City.

In May, 1933, Dillinger walked out of the prison, a free man for the first time in almost a decade. He was about to enter the eye of a crime wave that, for him, would be short and deadly. Few banks would be safe from him or other outlaws, who at times were better armed than the police.

They would continue to hit banks throughout much of the Midwest over the next eight months, until Dillinger and Pierpont were arrested in Tucson, Arizona. A few days later Dillinger was back in Indiana, his temporary home a cell at the Lake County Jail in Crown Point. Pierpont would be extradited to Ohio.

Years later, my dad would tell me of the empathy some men retained for Dillinger. A victim of the times, some said in that era before a criminal's background and shortage of incentives became an excuse for criminal acts.

Other men were disdainful of the crime spree, he said, and added that most of the men who sat around the barber shop, the general stores or Jerry Jones' feed mill in Heltonville agreed there might not be a jail that could hold Dillinger.

On March 3, 1934, The *Bedford Daily Mail* reported in 144-point type, "DILLINGER ESCAPES JAIL."

The United Press report began: "John Dillinger, notorious desperado and bank robber, broke out of the Lake County (Indiana) jail today and escaped in the private automobile of sheriff Lillian Holley."

Dillinger's daring act, perpetrated with a make-believe gun fashioned from soap and blackened with shoe polish, made the Indiana sectional basketball tournament that was underway a secondary story.

It was not surprising that some Dillinger sympathizers cheered as much for him as they did for their high school teams.

On July 23, 1934, *The Indianapolis News* told the story of Dillinger's demise: "Woman 'Tipoff' Sets Fatal Trap."

"THIRD EXTRA" read the type over an Associated Press story that recounted Dillinger's death from three gunshots fired by FBI agents outside Biograph Theater in Chicago on the night of July 22.

"The end of the incredible crime career of the internationally-known hoodlum," a subhead said.

To alert the FBI, Anna Sage, a female informant, had dressed in an orange skirt that would look red under the marquee lights, author John Toland noted in his book, *The Dillinger Days*. Agents watched as she, Dillinger and Polly Hamilton, his girl friend at the time, entered the theater.

They waited as the three watched Clark Gable in the movie "Manhattan Melodrama," ironically a crime story. Dillinger was shot as he left the theater, quickly abandoned by Sage and Hamilton, the Colt automatic still in his pocket.

The man who had terrorized banks across mid-America had $7.70 and a watch with a picture of Polly Hamilton in his pockets. In the end, crime had not paid. He had been betrayed by Miss Sage, who may have hoped to avoid deportation to her native Romania.

Back in Mooresville, his father told a reporter: "I suspect John would rather it had been that way. He never told me so, but they had laid so many things on him that I guess he would rather have been shot down than arrested again."

My dad recalled he had agreed. Mom said she had been more concerned about the hurt and pain his parents must have suffered when they heard the news of their son. It was true, she agreed, the innocent often become the victims.

No matter the era or the circumstance, the deaths of notable personalities—some good, some bad—are difficult for some to accept. For decades there would be rumors of Dillinger sightings around the nation.

In the 1960s we received a letter at *The Indianapolis News* signed "John Dillinger." The writer included what he said was his current picture, a snapshot of a man who appeared in his 60s.

The late Aldrich Harvey, who followed his dad Friday into the funeral business, said the picture resembled what Dillinger might have looked like at an older age, but added:

"We buried the right man (his dad had handled the funeral arrangements), noting both Dillinger's dad and his sister, in separate rooms, had drawn scars John had on his leg from a barbed wire cut as a teen on the farm. "The drawings were identical to one on the dead man's leg," Aldrich Harvey said, that fact killing what might have been a major news story.

The town of Mooresville—in its wisdom—has chosen yet today not to profit from the "Home of John Dillinger" label others have assigned to it. At the turn of the century it rejected a proposal for a museum in town. A few decades earlier, a new McDonald's Restaurant removed pictures of Dillinger from its inside walls after protests from citizens.

*   *   *

Except for minor thefts, public intoxication and a murder or two, we were unaware of any crimes or major trails that brought public attention to our area in the 1930s or the 1940s.

EDUCATION

Consolidation of rural high schools was four decades into the future when we entered a classroom for the first time. One-room schools remained open in our township at Henderson Creek and Hickory Grove, but the one at Zelma near our home had closed.

Educators at those schools also were the janitors, lighting fires in wood stoves before school, sweeping floors after classes. They were nurses, guidance counselors, art and music teachers, and playground supervisors.

That setting in which they taught permitted first graders to listen in on sixth grade classes, allowing the brightest of them to absorb knowledge beyond their years.

Church and school were not separated. I never attended the school at Zelma but I did, at my parents' command, attend revivals there on summer nights. Adults squeezed into student desks and listened to preachers spout the Gospel as they believed it to be. Children like me read the carvings on desk tops and dreamed of making bean flippers, bows and arrows and stick kites with newspapers.

High schools were small. Heltonville graduated 13 seniors in 1934, which seemed like a big class compared to the five at Tunnelton and the eight each at Williams and Huron.

Two county high schools, Fayetteville and Springville played basketball on outdoor courts until gymnasiums were built in the late 1930s.

Those austere circumstances may have bothered outside critics. They were accepted by those conditioned to depression and

hardship. It was a time when students expected little, yet appreciated what they received.

Pre-School Ritual

AUGUST 24, 1935: In a ritual of late summer, The *Bedford
Daily Times* reported that Lawrence County schools would open
for registration Friday and classes would start the following
Tuesday.

Lawrence Pierce, it added, would become principal at
Heltonville, replacing W.C. Roberts, who would move to Huron.
Roberts lived in Heltonville, high on a hill overlooking the east
entrance to town off Ind. 58. If there was a mansion in town it
was his long two-story frame house fronted by a manicured lawn.

The Roberts family was respected by residents, Roberts by
students. It made little difference for this was a time before
school consolidation, a time when township trustees hired and
fired principals and teachers on personal whims, often disregarding the advice of parents and county school superintendents.

School would be a new experience for me and other
six-year-olds. Kindergartens were what city students, not those in
rural townships, attended. Our pre-school classes were informal,
taught by older siblings who shared their advice and provided
insight on what to expect.

The transition from home to school was more anticipated
than dreaded. Only the adjustment to the confinement of classrooms was abrupt. The school at Heltonville had no indoor
plumbing, but neither did our homes. Restrooms were down cin-
der paths to big outdoor toilets, one, of course, shared by boys,
the other by girls. Teachers used the same accommodations.
Those restrooms would remain in place until after we graduated.

Our visits to indoor toilets were at the courthouse in Bedford
or when we visited relatives in town.

Frequency of visits to those outdoors facilities depended on
the temperature. Few tracks on their snow-covered paths were
visible when the thermometer dropped under 10 degrees.
Freezing toilet seats sharply reduced the pleas to be excused.

The school's main entrance at that time was off Ind. 58, which wrapped around the school yard in a hairpin turn. Stairs led down to the gymnasium, up to the second and third floors. Classrooms floors were pine, tongue and grooved and oiled by the janitor several times a year. Heat came from a giant coal-fired furnace through steam registers, which banged and clanged, sometimes louder than chagrined teachers could talk.

Desks had inkwells cut into the slanting top, accented by grooves for pencils. The back of the seats were the fronts of those behind them.

Each desk had a compartment under the top to keep books and lunch boxes, there being no cafeteria . . . and no vending machines. Our lunches were often peanut butter and jelly sandwiches, which looked sumptuous to compared to fatback in biscuits some others brought.

Blackboards stretched across the front of each room. Lockers at the side were to store coats, overshoes and whatever teachers could not fit into their desks.

The playground, a mixture of grass and cinders, had few rides, and opportunities for enjoyment at recess depended on the ingenuity of the pupils who seldom lacked for ideas.

It was into this setting we enrolled for the first time that Friday to find our classroom, meet the teacher and receive our book lists.

The Saturday that followed was a day like no other, not for us, not for our parents, not for merchants in Bedford. City schools there would not open until later, leaving the Courthouse Square to country bumpkins like us. Into town, we went with our parents and siblings, joining almost every county family in the purchase of texts at the always packed bookstore, bib overalls, cotton shirts, shoes and other apparel at crowded stores like J.C. Penney's and Keller's.

Most stores offered sales. Merit Shoes that week advertised "growing girls Oxfords, $1.49 a pair, boy's dress shoes for $1.49." We didn't need dress shoes. We got one pair to be used for school, church and chores . . . for an entire year. Durability and price always outweighed style and sometimes comfort.

School was a welcome bonanza for merchants, a regretful deflation of bank accounts for parents, who seldom complained. Most would have spent more if they had the money.

Cowboy actor Buck Jones was starring in "Blazing Guns" that day at the VonRitz Theater, but we would wait to attend the free outdoor movie that night in Norman.

The long Labor Day weekend allowed us to appreciate our new clothes and to open school books that emitted a welcome smell of newness that sharpened our eagerness to learn. We looked forward to the start of classes.

The Beginning

Our first grade teacher was Jessie Lively, a living institution, who had taught the only first grade the school had for what seemed like decades.

Experience had taught her that firmness was necessary to change ragtag and rowdy 6-year-olds into attentive students worthy of promotion into the second grade eight months later.

It was a tribute to her ability, patience and perseverance that she usually succeeded.

No class, probably, challenged her patience—or her ability—more than the 20 of us in her class that year. We didn't look like urchins the first day or two. We wore clean clothes, our hair was combed, our faces freshly scrubbed. It was always that way with each new class and Miss Lively knew it was an impression that would not last.

Each boy it seemed wore Big Mac bib overalls and work shoes. Most girls wore homemade dresses, a few had on outfits from J.C. Penney's.

The family names were familiar to her as she called the roll . . . "Bob Bailey. . . Betty Blackwelll . . . Leonard Chambers, down the list, finishing with "Edna Turpin . . . Billy Wray."

In two days, she knew each of us without her seating chart. In a week, she was aware of who would need special attention in order to learn and who would likely misbehave.

Teaching for her was easy. She needed no lesson plan. She proceeded at a pace equal to our ability to learn. No one was more delighted than she when each student comprehended what she taught.

Discipline was more difficult for her. The girls caused few problems. They had learned from their mothers. Boys had learned to romp free and unrestrained on farms with only occasional lessons in group behavior. Pranks were as much a part of our lives as the peanut butter sandwiches we carried in our lunch boxes.

No matter. I had avoided trouble until Dorothy Kinser showed up one day with a giant bow on the back of her dress. Sitting in front of me, that bow was too much of a challenge, too huge to sit there and ignore. I gingerly untied it, wrapped each end around the back rest of her seat and reknotted the cloth that still remained.

Once the bell rang, Dorothy lunged once, then twice, and a third time trying to stand. She stayed put.

Miss Lively rapped my hands with a ruler and sentenced me to three days without recess.

Sooner or later all of us were disciplined for one prank or another. To our credit we each learned in time good behavior was easier than the consequences for bad conduct.

When we returned as second graders the next September, Miss Lively watched smilingly as we traipsed into Ann Mark's second grade room. She turned and stepped into her own room, knowing exactly what to expect from another first grade.

That first grade (1935-1936 at Heltonville) was memorable, too, because of the weather. The worst blizzard in 20 years caused school to be dismissed when buses could not run. Snow was followed by a drop in temperatures that plummeted to 15 to 20 degrees below zero. Another blizzard hit on Feb. 12, climaxed by temperatures that fell to 18 below. I was six, but I still recall snow drifts as high as the school bus.

Summer went to the opposite extreme. It was 110 degrees on July 10 amid 10 straight days when 100-plus recordings were recorded.

I believe it was that fall, or the fall of 1937, when winds carried dust storms from the southern Great Plains. I recall seeing the skies fill with silt and coat the school bus with dust so heavy it had to be cleared by the windshield wiper.

Year 1937 was eventful because of the great flood that came after heavy rains. More than 17 inches fell in Lawrence County from Jan. 1 to Jan. 25, but the area was fortunate to escape the devastation that ravished the Ohio River valley. The Greater Louisville, Cincinnati and Evansville areas were underwater as were small Indiana river towns like Patriot and Leavenworth.

Newspapers on January 25 reported that 700 evacuees from the Greater Louisville area were at Spring Mill State Park and churches and schools in Mitchell. Another 700 to 800 were housed in Bedford.

At Heltonvile, older students helped the janitor set up bunk beds, sort blankets and prepare for homeless victims. I do not recall that any of the bunks were used, but even in depression years, Hoosiers were ready to help others.

A headline on January 17 noted the situation in Louisville: "Darkest Dawn in Her History."

Moving Ahead

Ann Mark as well as Esther Hunter, our third grade teacher, lived on farms in our area, attended the same church as we, and sometimes rode the school bus to class. Both were kind, but firm, and good teachers.

School at Heltonville was in recess for 30 days during the third grade when a major measles epidemic spread throughout the area. It was reported 134 of 475 students became sick. High school basketball games were canceled for a month and few families left home.

It also was the year scarlet fever kept me in bed and the rest of the family quarantined over the Christmas holiday. Miss Hunter, noticing I looked "peeked," sent me down over the hill to Dr. Jasper Cain's office. "Doc" took one look at me, reached for the phone and had the operator call my home.

He whispered, graphically, to Dad when he arrived: "Scarlet fever. Quarantine," the length of time forgotten. "Keep him in bed."

It was Friday, a few hours before the holiday break. My Christmas hopes fled from my dreams as fast as Santa's reindeer from a rooftop. I was sure I would miss the Yule treats Miss Hunter and the bus driver would give to students. I faced what I was sure would be the worst holiday of my young life.

It would, however, be one of the best. Both the teacher and bus driver had given my brother and sisters my sacks of candy, peanuts, oranges and tangerines. I was pampered, not hassled, by those siblings, the center of attention, not derision, for a few days. It ended when my sisters realized no boy friends could call until the quarantine ended.

Wilbur Wright was just out of college when he taught our fourth grade class. He too came from a rural background, easily adjusted to the classroom and made school fun. He started each day with song, leading us as we sang:

"I've got the joy, joy, joy
"Down in my heart, down in my heart,
"Down in my heart,
"Down in my heart to stay."

Once finished, he would direct,

"School days, school days
'Good old Golden Rule days,
"Readin', 'ritin, 'rithmetic
"Taught to the tune of a hickory stick."

If he ever used corporal, I don't recall it.

Wright made learning contagious. He cared about his students and became a friend for life, even though I disliked the role he gave me on the fourth grade basketball team. "You are the back guard," he said. It was a defensive position, one that meant—under his coaching—that I could never enter the offensive end of the court. I shot once, one time, the entire winter, that when I was fouled. I missed the free throw, proving teachers were indeed smarter than students.

Despite that basketball experience, he remained a friend for life.

Treasured Letter

Lawrence Pierce left as principal after that school year, when my older sister Nora was among 11 graduates. She and Pierce had developed a mutual respect even though they did not always agree. He was the principal, she the student, and she accepted his role.

In a letter mailed at graduation, she thanked him for the kindness he had shown, for the support he had given her and the other cheerleaders, for the guidance he had provided the Class of 1939.

"And most of all," she wrote, "I want to thank you for being my principal." She told neither her best friends nor anyone in the family. It was a personal message between a student and a principal, one whose meaning might be diminished if shared.

She received her diploma and went on her way through life as a wife, mother and beautician. By 1991, 52 years later, the incident was stored deep in the recesses of Nora's mind. Principal Lawrence Pierce has long since died. A letter arrived, a copy of a typewritten note attached. The letter was from the daughter of Lawrence Pierce, the typed note a copy of the letter Nora wrote in the spring of 1939.

Pierce had kept Nora's letter until he died. A son, then, had taken it to his home out west, bringing it back to Indiana when he came home to Bedford to retire. Together, through persistence, Mr. Pierce's son and daughter located Nora, who by then lived at Hanover, Indiana. And they let her know how much that simple message written 52 years before meant to their father . . . and to them.

Excellence is its own reward. For an educator, it is still nice to be told about it. . . even in 2003 when too many students never take time to do so.

Wrong Tune

We had other teachers, in the fifth grade, E. O. Winklepleck, who was in mid-career and a professional at what he did; in the sixth, Marshall Axsom, who would later be our high school basketball coach. He, too, would become a friend.

I received my first and only paddling in the sixth grade, not from Axsom, but from Mary K. Faubion, the music teacher. I was fooling around with a pencil when I blew into its small metal holder just as she walked into the door. The sound may have seemed like a wolf whistle to her, but I was too innocent to know what one was. Had I known, she certainly would not have been the object of any desire for she had never been the belle of any teacher's ball.

She grabbed my arm, yanked me into the hall and gave me three whacks with a paddle. She also gave me someone to blame for my everlasting lack of music appreciation.

Skunk 1, Fox 0

It was about that time our classmate Hubert Fox created even more excitement. Foxie had dressed for school when he moseyed out to see if he had caught any fur-bearing animals in the traps he had set the previous night. The traps remained open, but a skunk still at large doused a fleeing Foxie in its aroma. By then, the school bus waited and Foxie, grabbing his lunch pail, stepped aboard. He grinned as students already aboard grimaced.

Once inside the school, the scent spread. The principal demanded the janitor find "that confounded skunk that's loose in the building." A student seeking favoritism explained, "It's no skunk. It's Hubert."

By then, Foxie was in his seat. The principal burst through the door, red of face and sour of disposition, looked at Foxie and said:

"Hubert, would you mind telling us why you came to school reeking of skunk." If diplomacy had been a class Foxie would have received a grade of A and a score of 100. He replied:

"Well, sir, I just didn't have time to change clothes and take a bath in the washtub. And besides, you run such a fine school, I didn't want to miss a single minute."

The rest of us snickered for Foxie was not normally the most observant among us. The principal, unimpressed, said, "Hubert, you ought to know better than come to school smelling like you do."

Foxie had an answer for that, too. "They come to school if they've been told they'd be expelled for being late again."

The principal had heard enough. He ordered Foxie to "go home and don't come back until you get rid of that odor."

Foxie, happy for a day off from class, smiled from ear to ear and said, "See you tomorrow," leaving behind a reminder of the skunk he had encountered.

Fiery Graduation

As seventh graders we had different teachers, different classrooms, for each class. It also was the year the the nation entered World War II and life as we knew it changed forever. For students there would soon be an adversity closer to home.

APRIL 20, 1942: The *Bedford Times-Mail* headlined its top story: "Estimate Damage at $110,000 in School Fire at Heltonville."

It was not news to the 500 of us who were there the night before to attend commencement exercises. The superstitious blamed 13, the number of graduates, for the fire. The more reasonable considered other causes. Firemen never found its origin.

The graduates had walked onto the stage on one side of the gym, listened to Rev. J. E. Harbin give the opening prayer before entertainment by the school Glee Club.

Suddenly Sally Henderson, who lived nearby, ran into the gym shouting, "The school's on fire! The school's on fire!" Parents, relatives and friends of the graduates fled quickly, but orderly and without panic. The graduates followed, any processional quickly forgotten.

Outside, flames swept across the roof of the first section built in 1907, then spread to the gymnasium/classroom area added in 1925.

Men and boys entered and re-entered the burning building, salvaging records from the principal's office, typewriters and sewing machines from the commerce department, basketball uniforms from the dressing room.

Those uniforms were an omen. Teams from the school would play on another day, after a one-year absence. The diplomas for the seniors had been saved and would be presented, without ceremony, later.

Hundreds of spectators rushed to the school as the light illuminated the sky, hoping to help, the fire too hot for them to do so. Since the town had no fire department, a pumper truck, firemen Bill Robison and Ralph Williams aboard, arrived from Bedford. A 1,300-foot hose was laid down to Leatherwood Creek, the only source of water.

Author in junior high

Firemen saved the third section of the building, mostly brick and concrete in contrast to the kindling-like oiled floors and wooden inner walls of the older parts. Spectators slowly departed, a loss in their hearts, concern on their minds, doubt about the future.

Trustee Jack Clark, who estimated damage at $100,000, promised to work with O. O. Hall, the county school superintendent to determine where classes would be held the following year.

Clark said it was doubtful the war effort would allow immediate reconstruction and hinted some students might have to be sent to schools in nearby townships. It was a possibility none of us wanted to face.

We returned to the school the next day to look over the destruction. The older sections of the building were in ashes, smoldering amid warped steel girders in the basement, part of which had been the gymnasium. The chimney, which remained, towered unsupported over the still-warm rubble.

Each of us would spend the summer awaiting news about the next school year. Meantime, the saved section of the school was cleaned and prepared for use by high school students.

We in junior high would attend classes in the basement of the Heltonville Christian Church. Elementary pupils were to be in a rented building and the Oddfellows Hall and in a privately-owned building. Nobody objected for we all were relieved not be sent to another school system.

*   *   *

We knew by then the school would not be rebuilt until the war ended. We tried to study, but we felt confined in the basement classroom.

That's why we almost cheered when principal Raines visited the class one afternoon to ask for volunteers to help clean debris from the site of the school ruins. "We can sell the metal we salvage, make some money for the school and help the war effort at the same time," he said.

The next day each of us walked up the hill from the church, jumped into the basement and went to work. In the days that followed, we salvaged bricks and cleaned them of mortar, struggled to lift steam radiators, and located desk legs, twisted pipes and melted typewriters. The scrap-iron pile grew until it was hauled away to a place we were sure it would be turned into materiel of war.

Winter of Discontent

The winter ahead was long, dark, void of little good news, filled with uncertainty and void of many pleasures.

There was little to look forward to for teenagers around Heltonville. There would be no gym for practice or for games. Gas rationing was about to start, tires were to be limited and the thoughts of most adults were on the fighting in the South Pacific and in North Africa.

Teens, however, when not listening or reading the war news, were thinking of the basketball season ahead. They had expected that, somehow, some way, a basketball schedule would be played, even if the team had to practice outdoors and play all games on the road.

It was not to be. Principal Loren Raines announced in early October the grim news there would be no basketball that season. Some upperclassmen, who would have been on the team, chose to quit school and enlist in the military. Underclassmen, dismayed and disillusioned, stayed in school, their enthusiasm drained. School spirit dropped to a new low.

Meantime, a Bedford newspaper reported Shawswick also would forego the season ahead because of the war. The paper soon retracted its premature report, blaming its unnamed source for the error. "There will be basketball," the Shawswick principal emphasized.

Meantime, on October 30, the United Press revealed that the Indiana High School Coaches Association had drafted a letter to President Franklin D. Roosevelt asking that provisions be made to allow high schools the gasoline and tires needed for the transportation of athletic teams.

Signers of the letter included Ed Diedrich, Broad Ripple; Henry Bogue, Washington (Indianapolis); Russell Julian, Shortridge; Henry Orner, Crown Point; Paul Newman, Lebanon, and Clyde Lyle, Rochester.

They said coaches of America wanted to continue to turn out fighting men, and asked: "Will we have to scrap our athletic games when these games are the very instruments of basic training for our future fighting men?

"If necessary we advocate taking the required tires off beer trucks and using the necessary gas to transport our teams in order to play games.

"It is an established fact that the War Department is not satisfied with the type of fighters that the draft secures in the upper age bracket. This dissatisfaction is based upon our physical condition and poor mental attitudes. Our highest ranking officers have long pointed out the excellence of athletes for the fighting forces because of their fine physical condition and their will to win."

Meantime, schools began to adjust to the situation. Some limited the number of games, others readjusted schedules to eliminate long trips. A few, like Tunnelton and Huron in Lawrence County, reduced the number of games to eight, the minimum allowed for participation in the IHSAA basketball tournament.

At Heltonville, only patriotism remained high. The sports pages were distressing, the pre-season write-ups about other Lawrence County teams demoralizing for, not only Heltonville teens, but the adult fans around town. It made no difference that schedules for other schools had been limited, that the annual county tourney had been canceled or that many coaches had gone to war.

The year passed slowly. A few teens, who could find a ride with someone who had gasoline to spare, traveled to nearby schools to watch games.

February came at last, a few, warm days bringing hints of green to the grass, burning off the gloom that had blanketed the winter. It was time for the basketball sectional, a time for those around Heltonville to cleanse themselves of a regretful winter and enjoy the action at the "Quarry," the gym where the Bedford Stonecutters played.

They were a losing chorus as they cheered for the county teams against the county seat Stonecutters, hoping for an upset which was not to be when Oolitic fell short 28-25, on Saturday afternoon. Bedford went on to defeat Needmore, 54-36, for another of its many championships.

The sectional settled, county fans made Bedford their team, their horse to ride. And it would be a long ride, indeed. The Cutters won the regional, then defeated Evansville Central and Jasper in the semifinals at Vincennes.

We listened over the radio as a Final Four sportscaster gave the starting lineups for the Bedford game, Lebanon, Houser,

Again, Mount, Laflin and Truitt for Lebanon; Bedford, Wagner, Bellush, Brennan, Simmons and Beretta.

Only the static interrupted our concentration. John Brennan countered each Lebanon basket until Joe Hunter came to his aid with a couple of baskets late in the game, which went into the final minute, the winner uncertain.

"It's over," declared the announcer. "Lebanon wins, 36-35."

Bedford's adopted fans slumped into their chairs, recalling each missed basket, each unsuccessful opportunity to score. Brennan had netted 21 points to earn selection to most all-state teams. (He would later become an all-American at Notre Dame and in this year of 2003 was inducted into the Indiana Basketball Hall of Fame.)

My brother Wayne and I turned off the radio and headed for the barn. Much of the hay was gone, devoured by the livestock, leaving the loft smooth in front of the goal at the east end of the barn.

It was time to start practicing basketball again, although the next season was eight months—or maybe an eternity—away.

It mattered little to us when Fort Wayne defeated Lebanon for the state championship that night. Those were cities to the north, far from Bedford and places we knew.

*   *   *

Thanks to men like Marshall Axsom, the sixth grade teacher who became coach, Shorty White, and one or two other fans who used their rationed gasoline for trips, Heltonville played an abbreviated schedule of games the next season.

Despite the shortage of gas and tires, sports were vital to the education of teens and to their interaction with students from other schools.

It would be six years before a gym would be built and the Bluejackets would no longer practice at Shawswick and play all games on the road.

Looking back over those 60 years, it now seems those basketball seasons without a home gym were minimal sacrifices compared to that of older Americans who fought and died to win

World War II. As they are now, teens then were more wrapped up in their own self interests than in events that surround them.

Basketball was a diversion from the routine of our rustic lives. We lost more often than we won, but basketball remained a diversion from the routine of our rustic lives.

Hooping It Up

Basketball games were social events, uniting communities on Friday nights, allowing fans to forget for a time depression, war or whatever the concern of the time and the hour. Fans were rabid, their disdain for the opposing team matched only by their disgust with referees.

Each hamlet with a high school and at least five boys had a team. Games were played in cracker-box gyms with few seats, standing room only, crowd toeing out-of-bound lines. The sideline on one side of the playing floor at Shawswick was no more than two feet from the brick walls. Eight or ten rows of seats were on the floor and balcony levels.

Only gymnasiums at places like Bedford and Seymour had dressing rooms with showers. Visiting teams dressed in a band room at Clearspring, in a small cubicle at Freetown, in class-rooms at most other schools. A former Morgantown player recalled having to walk outdoors through snow from the Nash-ville gym to the visiting dressing room clad only in his basketball uniform and sneakers.

The gym at Freetown looked like a barn, seats in stall-like recesses off the playing floor. At Smithville, students perched on the stage at one end were known to rock the backboard when the opposition shot.

Teams seldom lost at home, the officials often "homers" hired at the will of school officials. Some referees, knowing the meanness with which rivals played, used a "no blood, no foul" approach. The pay for officials was small and it was not too rare to see one work a game by himself when a partner was a no show.

No matter how small the gyms, we envied each one of them as we had ever since our gym and school burned.

Political Game

A year after the Heltonville gym burned, a fire destroyed the school at Williams on the opposite side of the county.

Instead of finding makeshifts classroom as we did, Williams students were sent across White River to arch rival Huron, another small Spice Valley Township school. The Williams-Huron teams became one, the Williams players dominating the lineup for the 1943-44 and 1944-45 seasons.

The result—despite a better winning record than usual—did not set well with Huron fans who, it was surmised, would prefer for the Williams students to be sent back across the river from which they came.

From out of the darkness of war came an announcement in the *Bedford Times-Mail* in mid-1944.The Williams school would be rebuilt and with it a new gym. Heltonville students and fans were irate. Some suspected U.S. Rep. Earl Wilson was involved.

Wilson was a Huron native, with enough longevity in Washington to carry a big club loaded with clout. They suspected his friends back in Huron, as well as his backers in Williams, had convinced him to find federal funds to rebuilt the Williams school.

The results satisfied both constituencies. Williams would have its own high school again; Huron players would again be the real Beavers, not those intruders from Williams.

Heltonville had no ally in Congress, no political godfather. Its gymnasium would not be rebuilt, at least not with Wilson's help. One man's vote in Heltonville didn't mean as much as one man's vote in Huron or Williams.

In an ironic twist, the Heltonville "gymless wonders," as sportswriter Al Brewster sometimes called our team, played the Bulldogs of Williams in the first game ever in their new gym in November 1945. Politics had given Williams a new school and a sparkling new gym. It couldn't buy a basketball victory.

Heltonville won the game, 25-23. It was a sweet triumph but it did not help us get federal help to replace our gym.

Tying One On

Newspapers from Boston to San Francisco carried the story: "Indiana high school basketball game ends in a tie. Tunnelton 36, Heltonville 36."

When players from the two long-abandoned schools meet, decades later, they still consider the game a tie. It gave them attention more intoxicating than a victory. And now, the rest of the story.

The date February 8, 1946, a time when almost every Indiana hamlet was identified by their high school and their basketball team. The closer the schools were geographically, the more heated the competition.

Heltonville and Tunnelton were close, within eight or ten miles apart, across a few hills and hollows, separated by U.S. 50. As usual, the Tunnelton gym was packed, the three rows on each side filled, leaving fans standing in the corners and at each end. Neither team was having a great season and each saw the game as a chance for a victory.

It was a time before digital scoreboards, clocks that showed time by the seconds, horns that blared over the noise of the crowd. A faint whistle, blown by the timekeeper, was the only signal that time had run out.

The two coaches, Wilbert Gilstrap of Heltonville and Lester Gilstrap of Tunnelton, were brothers, good men who were better teachers than basketball mentors. They had agreed to take over the teams in World War II, and although the fighting had ended, young coaches had yet to be mustered out of service.

It would be a night when brotherly love would exceed the bitterness of a hardwood rivalry. It was game time! Heltonville took an 8-7 lead at the end of the first quarter and was ahead, 19-13, when Haden Crane of Tunnelton hit from the field as time expired. Despite protests by Shorty White, the Heltonville scorekeeper, and Irvine East, the timekeeper, the basket was counted.

It seemed unimportant at the time. Heltonville remained ahead, 26-19, when the fourth quarter began. Suddenly the momentum turned. Tunnelton came back to lead 38-36, the disputed basket by Crane the difference. Time was running out when a Heltonville player hit from the field, a basket that, if counted, would send the game into overtime.

Again an argument broke out. Tunnelton's official scorer and timer claimed the basket came six seconds too late. The Heltonville scorer and timer disagreed.

The referees, unable to detect when the clock had expired, left the decision to the official scorer and timer. Being from Tunnelton, they, of course, waved off the basket. Tunnelton fans left, thinking the Indians had won.

Wilbert Gilstrap sent us Heltonville players to the locker room to don our street clothes. He, brother Lester, and the timers, scorers and referees went into a conference and remained there when we walked to the school bus. It seemed like 40 minutes before coach Wilbert rapped on the door.

"What happened?" we shouted in unison. "We've decided to call it a tie game," he said, explaining that neither Crane's basket at the half nor the Heltonville shot at the end of the game would count. There would be no overtime, no replay, he said.

"Tie game," one player shouted. "That ought to make the papers tomorrow. "

Coach Gilstrap disagreed. "We decided not to report the game," he said, "we" being he and brother Lester. He didn't explain the reason for the news blackout, but the players assumed it was to maintain harmony in the two towns. Tunnelton players also were told the game was a tie.

Our bus headed northwest toward Bedford where we were given 35 cents each, as I recall, for a soft drink and sandwich.

Four of us agreed it was a story too good to be left untold. We asked Gilstrap for the scorebook, noticed the Tunnelton score still added up to 38 and erased two points from Crane's first-half total.

At Bedford, we bypassed the restaurant where the team had stopped, walked a block to the *Bedford Times-Mail* office and opened the book for sports editor Al Brewster. "Tie game," we told him.

Brewster knew a good story when he saw one. He copied the box score and headlined his report the next day: "Scoreboard error results in tie basketball contest." In hours, both the Associated Press and United Press had picked up the story.

It wasn't until the following Monday that Tunnelton fans disputed the story. Clifford Flinn, the timekeeper and scoreboard operator, informed Brewster:

"The reason for the tie was that after the game, the referees, timekeepers, scorekeepers and coaches met. The Tunnelton referees and timekeepers said there was no doubt but that Tunnelton won. The Tunnelton coach said, 'In order to have no hard feelings we will just call it a tie.' That's where the tie came in."

Flinn's comments left Brewster wondering: "How come they decided to call the game a tie if the referees and timekeeper said Tunnelton won? And how come the Heltonville scorebook had the two teams each with 36 points, 14 field goals and eight free throws?" Brewster's column remained a forum for debate for

1946-47 Heltonville basketball team. (Front row) Bill Ford, Bill Marlott, Bob Bailey, Wendell Trogdon, Tom Gilliatt, Gerald Whitted. (Back row) Bill Wray, Leonard Chambers, Coach Gilstrap, manager Frank May, Donald Todd, Ralph Sherrill

three more days, the two coaches remaining silent, above the fray. It mattered not to them, it seemed, who won or who lost. Brotherly love had triumphed over competition.

The two teams remained in the spotlight for a week, ending complaints that Brewster sometimes neglected county teams while covering the Bedford Stonecutters. The situation had changed. Tunnelton and Heltonville had received statewide recognition for a week. The Stonecutters had been rarely mentioned.

If Wilbert Gilstrap suspected the four of us who met with Al Brewster he never mentioned it to us. None of us ever mentioned who erased the one Tunnelton basket.

And Brewster, true to his profession, never revealed who brought him the scorebook. We continued to enjoy his wit and his sports coverage until he retired.

Foul Mood

As underclassmen some of us became adept at finding ways to get playing time. I had a gimmick that worked twice before it was detected. The first came after my brother Wayne was called for a personal foul.

"Better let me go in for him," I told coach Gilstrap. "That's his third foul." Gilstrap nodded in agreement. Wayne was livid as he came off the floor, uttering a few unkind words about the so-and-so coach. I can't recall how long he was on the bench but he wasn't happy gathering splinters.

The stunt had worked once, so I tried it again. Again my brother seethed as he walked by the scorekeeper to learn the foul was his first. Both the coach and Wayne had been conned again.

Gilstrap, hiding the humor in being scammed, assigned the student manager to track fouls. A new ploy would be needed to get more playing time.

In The Chips

There were no fall sports at Heltonville when we were in school. The high school did not have enough players for a team or enough money to buy uniforms and equipment. The hills were too steep and the dogs too mean for anyone to volunteer for a cross country team.

Besides, most of us got enough exercise running to back pastures to bring in the cows or chasing hogs that had strayed underneath fences in pursuit of freedom.

Baseball was a possibility, but the school didn't have any gloves or mitts and only two or three of the students had their own. A few of the guys like Bob Hudson and Howard Fox had enough calluses on their hands from hard work to handle line drives, but most of the others would have had trouble fielding lazy Texas Leaguers without gloves.

In the fall of 1944 coach Axsom scheduled softball games with Shawswick and Fayetteville even though there was no diamond on school grounds.

We found a level place in a pasture at the edge of town beyond a ravine and a fence. More than one of us ripped holes in our overalls and were smacked in the face by briers and limbs en route to the makeshift diamond.

Dried cow chips were used as bases the first couple days of practice. Axsom said he didn't think that was what Abner Doubleday had in mind and found three flat boards as replacements.

Fresh chips remained in the outfield. At least one player, going for a fly ball, slipped on a fresh dropping and ended up with embarrassment on his arm and pant leg. He cleaned up the best he could at the creek.

As I recall our first game was against Fayetteville. We were not discouraged by our two-run loss or criticized for our looks because the visitors also wore school clothes instead of uniforms.

The game with Shawswick was different. Called the Farmers, the team showed up with T-shirts that were all alike, laughed at the "path" to our diamond and complained they should have practiced at a dairy farm to be accustomed to the surroundings.

Anyhow, Shawswick won something like 21-3. In an understatement, Axsom said we were outgunned. He could have added outhit, outfielded and outclassed.

When a player asked about future games, coach Axsom suggested it was time to start thinking about basketball.

There were no more softball games that year. Axsom moved on to a principal's job in Rush County and Wilbert Gilstrap took over as coach the next fall. Asked about softball, he replied:

"I think we'll pass up the sport this year." None of the students who had played the year before complained.

Teaching Truths

Irvine East was the sternest—and the best—teacher we had in high school. The son of a blacksmith he had graduated from Heltonville in 1922 and could forge the minds of students as well as his dad could a horseshoe.

He tolerated no nonsense, yet he listened, slow to judge and liberal with his wisdom. He knew history and government and stressed their importance. No one passed his classes without an in-depth review of the Declaration of Independence:

"When in the Course of human events, it becomes necessary for one people to dissolve the hopes and expectations which have connected them with another."

Looking back, it could have been any of his students reciting the words, that document that capsulated a nation's hopes and expectations, in the 1930s and 1940s.

East required each student to memorize at least the first two paragraphs of the Declaration, as well as the preamble to the Constitution, and, to make sure they had done so, to say them in front of the class.

". . . and to assume among the powers of the Earth, the separate and equal station to which the Laws of Nature and of Nature's God entitle them. . . ."

Sometimes the students complained at recess or after school about how hard his classes were, calling him "Biggin."

But it was a term they used with respect in deference to his size. The students could have memorized the words and disregarded their meaning, but East saw to it that wasn't the case.

He taught them—or at least many of them—to dissect the sentences, to examine their meaning, to realize their significance.

To have done otherwise would have betrayed the obligation East had placed on himself to make each student a better citizen.

"... *A decent respect to the opinion of mankind requires that they should declare the causes which Impel them to the separation.*"

The students would pause, waiting to start the second paragraph of the Declaration, knowing it was easier to recite.

And East knew it held more meaning to them because it summarized the aspirations of what America was meant to accomplish. It gave hope to the poorest of the poor, for few, if any, of the students were born of wealth or position.

It let them know they need not be shackled to the chains of mediocrity, that they had at least a chance to reach, to at least dream, to try—if not to accomplish.

"*We hold these truths to be evident, that all men are created equal, that they are endowed by their Creator with certain unalienable rights, that among these are Life, Liberty and the pursuit of Happiness.*"

These were words the male students remembered when Japan attacked Pearl Harbor.

These were words that stayed with them through World War II, words that gave them a reason to fight the enemies of freedom in North Africa, Italy, France and from one island to another across the Pacific toward Japan.

These were words that gave some semblance of sense to the war for the students who still were to learn the lessons East was to teach.

The war ended, the Declaration again was safe from the threat of those who would take it away. And East continued to stress the value of knowing its content.

"*That to secure these rights, Governments are Instituted among Men, deriving their Just powers from the consent of the governed...*

"*... That whenever any Form of Government becomes destructive of these ends, It is the Right of the People to alter or to abolish it, and to Institute new Government...*"

It was difficult to tell who was the most pleased as the student neared the end of his recitation. The student, others in the class and East all smiled.

"... laying its foundation on such principles and organizing its powers in such form, as to them shall seem most likely to effect their Safety and Happiness."

As the student continued, East would remove his wire-frame glasses, clean the lenses and wait until the last words:

"To prove this, let Facts be submitted to a candid world."

He would look directly at the student and say, "Good." It was the best reward a student could ask for at the time. Each would hope for the same approval when it came time to memorize part of the Constitution.

*   *   *

Ruth Clark also grew up in Heltonville, graduated in 1918 and returned to teach. She tried to teach proper English to students who didn't hear it at home and manners to those of us who needed them. Yet she could be easily distracted.

A complaint about war rationing, a question about a world event would be the end of whatever lesson plan she had. Other teachers complained at times she was more of a friend than teacher to her students.

What she taught was not visible, like the items students made in Loren Raines's shop class or cookies baked in Miss Phegley's home economics room.

Much of what she taught, somehow, found its way into the recesses of the mind, to emerge unexpectedly later when reading a good novel, writing a letter, spelling a word or phrasing a sentence.

Ruth Clark died a few years before the high school at Heltonville closed and students were sent to consolidated Bedford North Lawrence where classes were structured and more formal.

She would not have liked that. Such formality was not her style.

Principal Partisans

Loren Raines, who had followed Lawrence Pierce as principal years before left Heltonville after our sophomore year and was succeeded by Howard Griggs.

Students considered Griggs a good principal and had no complaints about him. They had assumed he would be rehired for another year.

Griggs, like Raines, was a no nonsense principal. He may not have been as smooth in his manner or as respectful of elected authority, however. He gave few favors and asked for none.

He was authoritarian. The students knew what they could get by with, which was very little. He was fair and impartial. He had no favorites.

Those were the traits that won the respect of the students and the animosity of some folks who thought the fact they paid taxes entitled them to dictate policy.

Nobody knew for sure why the Pleasant Run Township trustee decided to terminate Griggs' employment. Some said he wanted to rehire Raines, who did come back the next fall as Griggs' replacement.

Whatever the reason, the decision to make a change came in early April, just a couple of weeks before school was out for the summer. Seniors, who were assured of graduation, took the lead in an effort to salvage the job for Griggs although they insisted they had no resentment toward Raines.

Griggs was not getting a fair shake they said. Underclassmen agreed. Griggs knew the politics of schools, held no grudge and would have discouraged the student effort if he had known about it in advance. Parents and other voting taxpayers signed petitions, which cited reasons why Griggs should stay on the job.

The senior males drove to the trustee's farm, stated the purpose of their visit and presented the petitions. They learned quickly the power of politics. The trustee looked over the petition, glanced through the names and told the students without rancor:

"A petition to me isn't worth the paper it's written on." He did not give a reason Griggs would not return, did not explain why the petition was meaningless. His message was clear. He was the power behind the school. His decision would stand. No amount of pressure would change his mind.

The students had tried and failed. They had bucked the system and come in second. They returned to their homes discouraged, thinking they had failed Griggs, themselves and the other students. They had lost the battle, but they had learned how to make an effort and the courage to oppose decisions they did not agree with.

Griggs left town that April knowing he'd made a lot of friends in just a year.

As expected Raines returned for our senior year.

Breaking Tradition

Loren Raines, was a minister as well as an educator. He also taught two or three shop classes and a Bible Literature class, during which, as I recall, he refrained from voicing his own religious convictions.

Had it been years later religion would have been all but banned from public schools and we could not know the value of his wisdom.

In contrast to Ruth Clark, Raines was not adored by students. I'm not sure I've ever forgiven him for breaking a long-established tradition in which senior players received the four tickets the school was allotted for the finals of the state basketball tournament.

The 1947 seniors had expected to be given the tickets as usual. We learned two days before the Final Four games that they would be used by Raines, his wife, and coach Wilbert Gilstrap and his spouse.

It was a cutting disappointment, even though my parents repeated again their "life isn't always fair" refrain.

An area farmer drove Bob Bailey and me to Indianapolis on game day in search of tickets to scalp. Prices were beyond our means. We ended the night at Shelbyville where fans celebrated their school's victory over favored Terre Haute Garfield. We likely had a more memorable day than our principal and coach, but we never let them know it was a day we enjoyed.

Lonely Day

None of the boys in class ever tried to curry favor. We were teens, eager to show our independence. I was attending a funeral one sunny spring afternoon when the other senior males decided to skip classes. When I returned the next morning, I was the lone boy in class. The others had been expelled.

It was a lonely discomforting experience, feeling alone and like a traitor to manhood. It was a relief when one of the parents convinced the principal to let the others return to class.

Quiet Ending

Our graduation was a simple ceremony held at the Methodist Church because the school still had no assembly or gymnasium.

There were no boisterous demonstrations by relatives, no shouts from friends, no inflated balloons as there would at commencements to come. It was a subdued event, befitting the depression and war that had been our companion over most of our dozen years together. We ended school as we began, anxious about a new era of life we faced with uncertainty.

The thirteen seniors in the Class of 1947 went their separate ways to seek whatever paths they would choose to follow.

Postmortem

I'm not sure what criteria Principal Raines used to rank students from top to bottom, but no one paid much attention to it.

It didn't matter, anyhow, until I drove down to Hanover College to meet the registrar. It was an era when World War II veterans filled classrooms and small colleges could be selective in the students they admitted.

We had talked for a while when the registrar asked where I ranked in my high school class.

"Sixth," I said, neither proudly or reluctantly.

We talked for awhile, before he comprehended I was neither swift of brain nor articulate of speech. "Just how many students were in your class?" he asked.

Told 13, he replied, "Oh." Even a country boy knew, "Oh" sounded like "Oh! No!"

I returned home, forgetting about college for a while. After spending the fall shucking corn and working on the farm, I enrolled at Franklin College, where, fortunately, the admissions officer did not ask about class rank.

THAT'S ENTERTAINMENT

Free Movies

In depression as in war, Americans need escapes. The 1930s and 1940s were no exception. Entertainment was varied, selective and much of it, fortunately, inexpensive.

Farm families in the depression found it at church socials, quilting bees and school events, on radio programs, in *Saturday Evening Post* stories and in books.

Preteens found joy among friends, in comic books and in fictional characters like Jack Armstrong, Buck Rogers and Joe Palooka, at cowboy movies in Bedford and sports events. Older teens, to their parents' disdain, sometimes visited pool rooms, sneaked smokes and listened to their elders at feed mills, general stores and barber shops.

All, no matter the age, usually gathered near C. E. Cummings' store in Norman each Saturday night from April to October.

It must have been about 1936, when C.E. showed the first talking picture show outside a theater in Bedford or Seymour. Some women, who may have noted the date, have long since died and their diaries destroyed, another bit of history cast aside by a younger generation.

Boys who were six or seven then can't remember the year, or the name of the movie. It certainly wasn't anything as classic as the *Jazz Singer*, the first successful talking motion picture, that had been shown in theaters in 1927.

The Norman talkie was a third-rate film at best. It was grainy, the sound unclear, voices out of sync with lips.

That was of no concern to those who had driven into Norman from miles around that Saturday night to see a free show. They came from Heltonville, Clearspring, Freetown and Kurtz and farms in between.

Most of them probably expected to see a silent movie, as they had every other Saturday night that summer. There was no theater in Norman, a town of 200 residents sometimes called Norman Station because Milwaukee Road trains once stopped there.

But C.E. Cummings didn't need a movie house for picture shows. He projected them onto a screen on the side of a building. C.E. was the town's leading merchant, an entrepreneur who ran a general store that sold everything from Aladdin's lamps, which created a white light from a circle wick that was far more illuminating than most kerosene lamps, to zinnia seeds with an assortment of items thrown in that would rival a Spiegel's catalog.

C.E. was part politician, part P. T. Barnum, a smart businessman who knew how to attract a crowd.

The script was the same each Saturday. He auctioned merchandise to the highest bidders from a dock on the west side of his store. It was a way to dispense dust-coated, slow-moving items and give customers a bargain in those days of depression.

Meantime, youngsters could spend their dimes in the store, five cents for a triple-dip ice cream cone, five cents for soda pop. C.E. ended each sale at dusk and the audience he had brought to town would find seats on cross-ties for the free movie.

There was no fanfare that night when the first talkie unwound.

C.E. never ballyhooed his movies, hadn't shown a preview of this one. The film flicked, scratchily, from "5" to "4" to "3" to "2" to "1" then showed the title. No one suspected anything but another silent picture.

Words came from the mouths of the actors. "It's one of them talkies we been reading about," shouted a woman who sat off to the side on a chair her husband had bought at the sale.

On the screen, a man spoke. "What'd he say?" asked a timber cutter, reaming out his ear with his right little finger.

It was a question that would be answered by a hundred voices, saying in unison, "He said . . ."

Viewers, caught up in the dialogue on the screen, repeated almost every line, every word. They seemed entranced, believing only they, not those around them, could hear the words.

"He said, '. . . .'," "She said, '. . . ,'" echoed across the barricaded street where the audience sat enraptured.

Lines were re-spoken even after "The End" froze on the screen. Adults and children were still doing "he saids, she saids" as they walked to their cars.

C. E. would bring a hundred or more talkies to Norman and the audience's repetition of lines would fade. Somewhat. But not completely. "He said, '. . . .' "She said, '. . . .' " would continue to accent each movie.

Matinee Mania

As we grew older we found rides to Bedford where we watched the double feature, plus serial, that ran on Saturday afternoon at the Lawrence Theater that was beside the Monon tracks just south of Courthouse Square.

It was prior to World War II, a time when men were men, when life was simple and when good always triumphed over evil.

The movie good guys wore white hats, rode fast horses, righted wrongs and rid the West of dastardly culprits who sought to destroy the virtues of honesty, compassion and fair play.

The good guys were riding, roping and straight shooting cowboys like Wild Bill Elliott, Randolph Scott, Hoot Gibson, Ken Maynard, Tim McCoy and Tom Mix, who used their fists as well as their six guns.

There were cowboys like Lash Larue, who used a whip instead of a gun. And riders and ropers like Gene Autry and Roy Rogers, who sang songs and had sidekicks like Smiley Burnette, Gabby Hayes, and "Slim" Pickens and Pat Buttram.

And the Cisco Kid and the Durango Kid and young actors who claimed they were Billy the Kid.

There were so many cowboys we each could have our own hero. One friend liked Ken Maynard, a Hoosier who had left Columbus to become a movie cowboy. Others chose Tim McCoy, Randolph Scott, or William Boyd, who was Hopalong Cassidy in the movies.

One of my favorites was Bob Steele, a little tough guy who could whip men twice his size. Sometimes he was a bad guy, sometimes he was a good guy. But he always acted the same and he had a way with words, words like "dirty yellow-livered sidewinder" and "sniveling low-down slime," which I could use in fun on the school playground.

Steele always wore clothes that looked like they'd been slept in and belonged on the characters he played.

None of us cared much for Roy Rogers or Gene Autry. Like Hopalong Cassidy, they were always clean shaven with neat hair cuts, wore clean clothes and talked like school teachers instead of riders of the ranges.

Rogers and Autry were always stopping right in the middle of the pursuit of evil to pick up their guitars and sing mushy songs to pretty girls who just happened to show up on the stagecoaches from back East. Gene and Roy looked the women in the eye, held them at the shoulders and promised to return before sundown, which said something about their priorities.

They never did get around to kissing them, at least not in any movie we saw. Any semblance of reality was accidental.

In the second movie we could see Gene Autry shoot at a rock Roy Rogers had hit in the first. Once Rogers fired 15 shots from a six-shot revolver. When we laughed someone in our crowd joked, "When you're on the right side of the law you don't count. You just keep shooting." Gene and Roy cut the enemies off at what looked like the same pass, and then corralled them in what looked like the same dry gulch and jailed them in what looked like the same cell.

If we could, we went back the next Saturday, any diversion from the usual routines of our lives were welcome.

Fantastic Films

With the addition of sound, movies became increasingly popular. Comedies, gangster movies, and musicals helped people forget their troubles.

A few friends, usually children from small families that could afford tickets, attended Shirley Temple movies at theaters. Some saw "Snow White and the Seven Dwarfs," one of Walt Disney's early animated films, and "Wizard of Oz."

Teachers talked about seeing "The Hurricane" and "Captain Courageous," which premiered in 1937, but no movie until that time equaled "Gone With the Wind," which opened at the VonRitz Theater in Bedford on April 8, 1940. Historian James Guthrie noted that many of those who attended paid "an unheard of price of $1" for a reserved seat.

Clark Gable (as Rhett Butler) uttered "damn," which shocked many of the viewers. It would be an overly-mild expletive compared to the vulgarities that could be heard on movie screens and television sets in years to come.

"Gone With the Wind" was the long-anticipated movie based on Margaret Mitchell's book of the same name.

Once we grew older and earned money we often attended what was called "the midnight" show at the VonRitz or Indiana Theaters in Bedford. Long lines waited to buy tickets for the films that started at 11 p.m. Most features were forgettable, the news reels like "Time Marches On" and "RKO News" often more enjoyable and educational. One of the better pictures shown then, as I recall, was "Double Indemnity."

It was a period of great movies. Classics were numerous in the 1940s, among them "Casablanca" and "Citizen Kane." Others were "It's a Wonderful Life," "Maltese Falcon" and "The Treasure of Sierra Madre." Among our favorites was "The Best Years of Our Lives," a 1946 film that captured life's conflict for returning veterans.

"Sergeant York," a World War I picture, opened in 1941. It was prelude to numerous battle films about World War II that were produced in the 1940s. Among them "Sands of Iwo Jima" and "Wake Island." The war movies showed the casualties of war and made teens even more patriotic and eager to do their part to fight the enemy.

Cigarettes seemed to be a part of every movie. Male actors often smoked continuously, then were joined by stylish actresses who in turn influenced Americans to become addicted to the then unknown health hazards of tobacco. It was not unusual to see women copy the seductive poses of actresses with cigarettes as their props.

Phrases and buzzwords used in movies became part of our lexicon.

Saturday Night Out

Downtown Bedford belonged to the city on most days. It was "occupied," however, on Saturdays by rural residents of Lawrence County.

Parking spaces were at a premium. Each side of Courthouse Square was ringed with cars. Streets in each direction were crowded.

Once adults, who came to shop, pay property taxes and run errands, departed for home, young married couples, youths with dates, and teens occupied the void.

Once we became teens we turned our interest from the free movies at Norman to the attractions in Bedford, be they the sweets at the confectionery shop, a harmless game of pool at Kattis' in the basement of the Masonic Temple, or a movie.

Rivals from rural schools at basketball games became allies at night, the bonds that united them more mutual than any affinity they might have for teens who attended the big city school.

Shopping trends changed. Courthouse Squares no longer were centers for shopping, teens became adults, young couples married and stayed home and a new generation found interests other than a Saturday night trip to town.

Law offices, banks, title offices and investment firms took over storefronts on squares and merchants moved to retail malls with vast parking lots.

Television arrived in the late 1940s and reached rural areas in the early 1950s. Movies on big screens no longer were a main source of entertainment, but they would continue to be a part of the American culture although most theaters became movie-plexes away from the heart of cities.

Spare A Dime?

Juke boxes brought music to small town restaurants and soda shops, allowing music to be played for a nickel or a dime at a much better quality than could be heard over radios of that time. The devices, made by Wurlitzer and other companies, were floor models that could play selections listed on coin boxes on walls at booths.

Many of the boxes were called nickelodeons, a name first given to theaters in the early 1900s and to player pianos later. "Put Another Nickel In, In the Nickelodeon" became a popular song of the area.

Big bands, led by men like Glenn Miller, Tommy Dorsey, Duke Ellington and Benny Goodman, drew couples to dance floors and resorts across the nation. Despite its grammar, Ellington's "It Don't Mean a Thing If It Ain't Got Swing" was a hit with younger couples.

The jobless and desperate found relief from the Depression in the realism of songs like "Brother, Can You Spare a Dime?"

"They used to tell me I was building a dream,
        and so I followed the mob,
When there was earth to plow, or guns to bear,
I was always there right on the job.
They used to tell me I was building a dream,
with peace and glory ahead,
Why should I be standing in line, just waiting for bread?

"Once I built a railroad, I made it run, made it race against time.
Once I built a railroad; now it's done.
Brother, can you spare a dime?
Once I built a tower, up to the sun, brick, and rivet, and lime;

Once I built a tower, now it's done.
Brother, can you spare a dime?"

Songs such as "Life is Just a Bowl of Cherries," uplifted spirits. "We're in the Money" from the movie "Gold Diggers of 1933" was more upbeat than realistic, its lyrics reading in part:

"We're in the money, we're in the money;
We've got a lot of what it takes to get along!
We're in the money, that sky is sunny,
Old Man Depression you are through, you done us wrong.
We never see a headline about breadlines today.
And when we see the landlord we can
*   look that guy right in the eye.*
We're in the money, come on, my honey,
Let's lend it, spend it, send it rolling along!"

Broadway musicals for those with money and means included "Anything Goes" and "Red Hot and Blue," by Hoosier Cole Porter, and "Girl Crazy" and "Strike Up The Band" by George and Ira Gershwin.

Richard Rogers and Irving Berlin scripted songs that likely will never fade from American music.

Many of the 1940s songs, as movies, had patriotic themes. A soldier who sung "I'll Be Back In a Year" to his "little darling" would be gone for much longer and the tune would quickly fade as the war continued. Other songs with war themes were "Five Minutes More," "Anchors Aweigh," "I'll Be Seeing You," "Praise the Lord and Pass the Ammunition" and "Bell Bottom Trousers."

Among the popular songs were "I Can't Begin to Tell You," "I'll Walk Alone" and "Third Man Theme." The 1940s also saw great musicals, among them Rodgers and Hammerstein's "Oklahoma," "State Fair," and "South Pacific."

Big bands began to disband in the 1940s, leading Frank Sinatra and other vocalists to go on their own, many to become popular as recording artists and as singers on television shows and in movies.

By the 1930s, hillbilly and western music was becoming more popular, aided by singing cowboy movie stars and radio programs such as the Grand Ole Opry.

Old-time music seemed outdated in contrast to hillbilly songs that could be kept fresh with new lyrics and sounds. Attire and mannerisms changed as public appearances were required of singers whose images were often shaped by promoters.

The Opry, the National Barn Dance and other country type shows became weekend fixtures on radio and Roy Rogers and Gene Autry rode on to movie screens singing cowboy music.

It was said the new country music of the day evolved from a combination of western, string and gospel into an image that would have broad appeal in cities, in small towns and across all social strata. It was the kind of music rural youth could play on their string instruments and sing songs that related to their lives.

No star was more popular in the 1930s than Roy Acuff, who became labeled as "King of the Hillbillies" and "Caruso of Mountain Music" after songs like "The Great Speckled Bird" gave him instant fame. It was reported his music sold more records through the 1940s than any other country singer.

Meantime, the Carter Family was leaving its mark on country music but it would be the late 1950s before Patsy Cline rose to fame as one of the all-time favorite female singers with songs like "Crazy," and "I Fall to Pieces."

Bill Monroe appeared on the National Barn Dance aired on WLS radio in Chicago early in the 1930s decade and joined the Grand Ole Opry with the Blue Grass Boys. The Monroe sound was different, a mixture of old-time string bands with the blues, rural spirituals and jazz.

It was said the real bluegrass with the banjo sound did not take its full form until Earl Scruggs joined the group in 1945.

Some of the popularity of country music may have come because it seemed to retain the rural culture of America at a time of urbanization.

Novel Ideas

Despite the depression, the 1930s produced memorable novels that reflected the events of the time. John Steinbeck's *Grapes of Wrath* told the story of an Oklahoma family displaced from the Dust Bowl by the drought. In *Tobacco Road*, Erskine Caldwell dramatized the plight of poor blacks in the rural south. The story of blacks and the prejudices they faced was revealed by Richard Wright in *Native Son*.

The decade, too, saw the works of Thornton Wilder, F. Scott Fitzgerald, Ernest Hemingway and other authors as well as poets like Carl Sandburg and the whimsy of Ogden Nash whose work appeared in the *New Yorker.*

The rhymes of Dr. Seuss were en route to popularity.

Less noted writers, using "New Deal" grants, produced novels, historical studies and plays.

On The Radio

Evenings were the best part of the day in farm homes in the winters of the 1940s. World War II was being fought around the world, gas was rationed, and there were few places to go even if it had not been.

Into this seeming vacuum each evening came the programs that were as popular in their time as "The Simpsons" would be on television in the 1990s.

Young girls rushed into the house to hear "Little Orphan Annie" and "Terry and the Pirates." The boys raced up the hill and bounded into the house in time for "Jack Armstrong, the All-American Boy," "Superman" and "The Lone Ranger," who was so secret his pal Tonto didn't know his name." None of us wondered until later why an "All-American Boy" like Armstrong wasn't fighting for his country either in North Africa or the South Pacific.

But at the time, he and the Lone Ranger and Tonto were an outlet, an escape from a world filled with depressing news and little prospect it would get better.

The commercials plugged Wheaties, Ovaltine and other snacks that could be fixed in the minute or so the ads were aired.

Jack Armstrong was over by 5 p.m. and the next 45 minutes were spent on chores. The programming seemed designed for a typical farm family, or maybe the families tailored their lives to fit the programming.

It was an orderly arrangement. At least it seemed so. Dad would come into the house with an armload of wood and feed the stove in the living room, hang up his old denim coat, rip off his four-buckle overshoes, wash up, pull a chair over by the radio and switch the dial at 5:45 to Lowell Thomas.

Gabriel Heater and H.V. Kaltenborn, who came on later in the evening, were all right, but somehow they didn't give Dad the feeling that everything would eventually be okay like Thomas did when he said, "So long until tomorrow."

Mom had supper ready when the news was over so we could listen to the "Amos and Andy" show, which was set in New York's Harlem that was unfamiliar to us. The humor was good, though, and we laughed a lot with Kingfish and his "I's regusted" comments, Madam Queen, Ruby Taylor and Sapphire Stevens.

"Lum 'n Abner," though, was different. Dad said the show, supposedly set in Pine Ridge, Arkansas, could be about Heltonville because it had a similar set of characters. Even Mom stopped working long enough to listen to rustics Lum Edwards, Abner Peabody, Cedric Weehunt and Squire Skump. She ended up laughing as much as we did.

"The Lone Ranger" came on, as I recall, at 7:30 to the "William Tell Overture" and the thundering hoofbeats of the great horse Silver.

Once that show ended, the radio was turned off as soon as the Lone Ranger rode off for the night. The Rural Electric

Administration had not yet turned on the electric lights in our area and would not until 1948 or 1949.

Dad turned up the coal oil lamps and read the *Country Gentleman* or *Farm Journal* or the local newspapers. Mom mended clothes, crocheted or read the Bible first, then *The Saturday Evening Post*. We did home work if we had it, which was rare, our teachers being more lenient than they should have been.

Mom turned the radio each morning to a religious show called "Backsliders Brought Back" aired over a powerful station at Del Rio, Texas. The preacher spouted hellfire-and-damnation and condemned hard liquor so ardently he made Carrie Nation seem like a moderate.

Her favorite programs, "Mary Foster, the Editor's Daughter," and "Lorenzo Jones" came on in the afternoon when she could listen uninterrupted. She lived to see television, but she refused to the watch what she called "the silly soap operas."

Dad lived a month short of his 95th birthday, long enough to say "so long until tomorrow" to Lowell Thomas.

Most radio programs were broadcast from high-powered stations like WLW in Cincinnati and WHAS in Louisville. WBIW began operation in Bedford in the late 1940s and gave an immediacy to local news events.

*   *   *

Philco engineers demonstrated how television appeared on screens at the 1938 Indiana State Fair. It was not available on an Indianapolis station until May 30, 1948, when WFBM-TV televised the 500-Mile Race. By the end of the decade the grainy black and white shows would be seen in homes across central Indiana.

Diamond In Rough

Baseball was an enjoyable summer diversion in the late 1930s for rural youngsters too young to play. We listened when we could as Waite Hoyt broadcast Cincinnati Reds games over WLW and we spent every Sunday up the road at the ball diamond on Homer Duncan's Farm.

The games likely have faded into faint memories for the players on that Heltonville Merchants team who remain. But not for me and a few others. We still reminder as the reel of time rewinds in our memories.

We remember Harry Axsom, the fastball pitcher on the mound, and Marshall Axsom, his brother, behind the plate. We recall Cladie Bailey, the first baseman who pitched some when he wasn't playing for the Heltonville 400 team. And we remember the Lantz boys, Raymond and Earl. And other players like George Covey, the big guy who played first base when Bailey pitched, and Herbie Harrell, the little chattering second baseman, and Ed Cain and Bish Wagoner. And the manager, Shorty White.

Each of us pre-teen farm lads had our national baseball idols, Ted Williams, Joe DiMaggio, Bob Feller and others who were just moving into superstar status. We assumed we would never see them play. They were names in papers, pictures in *The Grit,* personalities mentioned on radio sportscasts.

Cladie, Marshall, Earl, Raymond and George were real. They wore uniforms with "Roberts General Store" and "Jones Funeral Home" on their shirts. They played the game, not for money or glory, but for the sheer appreciation of the sport.

The diamond was at the southeast corner of Ind. 58 and Back Creek Road. It was a big flat spot without an outfield fence. A home run was any long, fly ball the fielders couldn't reach. The infield was scalped and hard, and ground balls sometimes took crazy bounces. But the Merchants knew how to play the caroms and the errors usually belonged to the visiting team.

There was no running water and no wells nearby. The players drank water from a big five-gallon can or soda pop from a big tub filled with ice.

We usually brought 15 cents to the games, a nickel for the pop and 10 cents to put in the hat that was passed about the seventh inning to help keep the team funded.

The Merchants won more than they lost. And so did the Heltonville team called the 400s. The 400s had nicer uniforms, better players and attracted more attention from the two Bedford newspapers.

We were proud when the 400s brought recognition to the town when it advanced to the State Amateur tournament in Kokomo.

But the 400s weren't really an all-Heltonville team, even though they were managed by Bailey, who also played with Loren Henderson, Mack Todd, Dale Sowder, Ray Chambers, all of whom lived in town. The 400s' home diamond was off Ind. 58 in the Leatherwood Creek bottoms near the Milwaukee trestle and its old Shawswick Station.

By 1942 most of the players were in military service, the backstop was removed and the land farmed as it still is today. Each time we make the turn off Ind. 58 a faint echo of "Atta boy, Harry. Way to pop that pill," sounds within us and visions of another strikeout develops into a picture from the past.

Shopping Center

General stores were the convenience stops of the day, Lowe's Hardwares, Wal-Marts, Krogers, TSCs outlets. Whatever a family needed, stores like C.E. Cummings in Norman and R. R. Roberts in Heltonville had it, an exception being medical prescriptions. That was of no major concern for there seemed to be home remedies for every illness.

It wasn't necessary to say anything to enjoy the experience at the R.R. Roberts & Son general store in Heltonville.

The store was maybe 100 feet long, with a second building for feed and farm products in the rear. The walls of the front store were lined with merchandise on shelves that reached from floor to ceiling.

Up front, there were food staples on one side, clothing and footwear on the other. To the rear were meat and produce lockers, eggs, milk coolers and a cutting and wrapping table.

It was a one-stop store of the 1930s and 1940s. A farmer could buy anything from horseshoe nails to chewing tobacco to gumboots to pickled bologna.

It also was a good place to kill time, enjoy the conversation and learn any gossip being spread maliciously or with good intent. And there was no charge to just sit around the stove and listen and watch men like a man called Fritz.

Fritz, a farmer, came in about every week to buy a few groceries to supplement what his family had grown in the garden the previous summer.

When Bob Roberts got ready to wait on him, Fritz unbuttoned the bib pocket on his overalls, held the shopping list written on yellow note paper 30 inches from his eyes, squinted and called out each item he needed.

"One big box of Post Toasties," he said. Bob would repeat, "One big box of Post Toasties," pick up a device that looked like a long pole, walk down an aisle, squeeze the handle to open a clamp-like device that grasped the cereal near the top of a wall.

"Five pounds of sugar." Bob repeated, "Five pounds of sugar," and added, "38 cents."

Fritz griped, usually jokingly, "Thirty-eight cents. Man, that's seven and two-thirds cents a pound."

Bob knew he was being ribbed.

Once the staples were boxed Bob and Fritz walked back to the meat counter where Bob sliced a pound of cheese off a big round hunk, weighed it on the white Toledo scales, adding an extra ounce free for good measure.

He then pulled brown paper from a roller, wrapped the cheese, yanked a roll of twine from a spool and tied the package.

Back up front Fritz asked, "Got any rivets for harness? I need to fix some before the weather gets warm enough to hitch up the team again." Bob found the rivets in an alcove, then weighed them to determine the price.

He wrote each item on a 3 by 5-inch sales slip divided by carbon paper and asked Fritz, "Forget anything."

Fritz asked about hip boots. "It's mighty muddy out at the farm now that the thaw is here."

Bob climbed a thin ladder that rolled along the side of the store, pulled down two pair and said, "Either pair, $2.95."

Fritz looked them over and replied, "Sorry, Bob, too much. And by the way, I need five gallons of Red Crown for that puddle jumper of mine out front."

Red Crown was a grade of Standard gas in the gravity pumps "out front." The "puddle jumper" was Fritz' car. Bob Hunter, who worked at the store, pumped the gas while Bob added the bill.

He could banter as well as Fritz. He whistled, then said, "You got a doozy this time. Comes to $7.37. Wanta put it on your bill?"

Fritz nodded. "You'd better, I expect. Ain't sold that crib of corn yet and my hogs won't go to market for a couple more weeks."

Bob knew Fritz would settle his debts as soon as he had the money. He always did. Fritz picked up the merchandise Bob had boxed. "Much obliged, Bob." Bob would answer, "Not at all, Fritz. Anytime."

Fritz was smiling as he drove off. Knowing they were trusted to pay made men of the depression feel good.

Meantime, men seated around the stove a few feet from the cash register continued their conversation, uninterrupted except for a ping of tobacco juice on the metal coffee can.

Taste of Trouble

Bob Roberts could also be kind and forgiving, even if we did find entertainment and nourishment at his expense.

Four or five of us walked the four miles home from junior high basketball practice two or three times a week. We strolled down the hill from the school, stepped onto the railroad, tiptoed across a Milwaukee Railroad trestle and passed the post office toward the Roberts' Store.

It would be past 6 p.m. The store was closed and we were famished, making the unlocked Honey Krust box outside an invitation to our appetites for it always contained some unsold loaves.

We took turns each trip, dashing across a ditch, heisting a loaf from the box and sprinting back across the tracks that paralled Ind. 58. We shared the slices as we talked, each piece as scrumptious as if it held a tenderloin strip or peanut butter and jelly. Not a crumb would be left by the time the last person arrived home.

We all knew it was wrong to take the bread and agreed to admit our theft and offer to pay Bob for it. Somehow the right time to do that never seemed to come, at least it did not come soon enough.

We had no idea the bread had been missed . . . until Dad called me aside one night, saying, "I want to talk to you, son." When Dad wanted "to talk to me, son," I knew it was not for getting a B on my report card.

Bob, he said, had told him about our theft of bread loaves almost from the start. Dad had offered to pay for our take home meals, but Bob said, "Forget it. It was worth it to let them (us culprits) think we were getting away with something." Bob had called us "good kids" and said he knew we wouldn't have taken the bread if we weren't hungry. He had trusted us to learn from the experience.

"Don't ever let him down, or me either," Dad said. As far as I know, none of us did. We let Bob know we appreciated his trust. And we managed to walk home from then on without those savory loaves of Honey Krust.

Suffering Sulphur

Saul Barrett's sulphur spring was always good for a laugh. For us, that is, not friends from town who came out to visit.

The spring ran from a vein in the hill into a basin chiseled into the stone. Saul said the water was good, that "people spend lots of money to visit French Lick, West Baden, Martinsville and Trinity Springs." "Spas," he called those places, claiming the water from his spring had just as many minerals.

The sulphur water had a golden hue that dyed the moss and soapstone yellow as it flowed toward the basin. It was thicker than water, but it may have just seemed that way.

We told each friend we showed the spring that the water would grow hair on their chests and expand their muscles. We never told them how it tasted and they never asked why we weren't drinking it. None of them complained about the taste or the smell until the kid, we will call Joey to protect his image, came out from his home in town.

He took a long drink out of the dipper Saul kept at the spring and swallowed the water before the taste hit and the odor registered.

His comment echoed off the tin roof of Saul's small barn.

"Hell's fire," he roared. "This damned stuff is a combination of gunpowder and rotten eggs." He griped about it the rest of the day, and unfortunately, I paid him no heed when he promised to get even.

The threat had slipped my mind two weeks later. In the midst of a visit at Joey's house he handed me a glass that had about an inch of clear liquid in it. "Try this. It's something my Dad likes," he said.

In my naiveté, I swallowed it all. Once it hit bottom I grabbed my stomach, coughed, jumped like I was on hot coals and cussed up a storm that turned the air a lot bluer than the summer sky. I finally managed to ask Joey what it was.

"White lightning. Illegal alcohol. Just somethin' Pa keeps around for his friends," he explained once he stifled his laughter.

He didn't say what his dad served his enemies. I was just happy I was a so-called friend.

Ignorance Bliss

Pot, as far as most country boys knew, was a granite container their moms used to make coffee. It certainly was not, to their limited teen-age experiences of the early 1940s, a drug to be smoked for enjoyment or any other reason.

They seldom dared buy Marvels for eight cents a pack or Camels which cost a dime. Cigarettes, their parents and their coaches warned, would harm their bodies, stunt their growth and limit their stamina. They knew that before the surgeon general of the United States cited the danger 20 years later.

"Evil" . . . some fundamentalist ministers around Heltonville said of cigarettes.

No teen, at least those with whom we associated, dare light a smoke in sight of an adult. And marijuana was a word unfamiliar to them.

They grew toward manhood, consumed by the trials of adolescence, ever alert to the news that unfolded on the World War II battlefields around the world. They had little time to loaf or be idle as had jobless young men of the depression years of the 1930s.

It was just as well. Older adults with time on their hands might have exposed their younger neighbors to new experiences. Instead we remained free of any temptation we might, otherwise, have had. It would be years later before we knew that pot, even cocaine, had been available in that earlier decade.

It was news when we learned that marijuana was a drug of the depression, that 50 tons of the weed had been destroyed in Indiana as early as 1938. Or that smoking pot was on the increase in the years before America went to war, galvanizing an entire generation in a united effort.

News reel we had not seen called marijuana "the weed with roots in hell." We had turned to the comics and sports page in 1939, missing the news item that a marijuana plant had been found in Lawrence County. We had overlooked a *Prairie Farmer* magazine crusade which had campaigned against marijuana.

Nor had we read a history of Lawrence County, which reported a 1930s warning: "Dreaded opium is merely a sedative, compared to the danger of marijuana. Armies have been crazed and countless lives lost and debauched through its devastating effect on the brain." The history book recorded that "The Mexican weed" or "India Hemp" was used among college students more than others in the 1930s.

It seemed of little concern to us, that belated knowledge of a decade that preceded our adolescence. We had never missed what we did not know existed.

Ignorance was not a virtue, we decided, but neither had it been a vice. As we grew older "pot" did take on a new meaning.

Not as in marijuana, but as in the money on the table in an occasional friendly poker game.

When marijuana resurfaced again in the 1960s some people called it "a new threat." It may have been a threat, but it was not new.

The Chivaree

About the last thing you'd expect newlyweds to appreciate was a chivaree, one of the entertainment escapes of the period.

Especially Jesse and Fern. They weren't the type who liked to be center stage or to seek attention for themselves.They were a little older than most rural couples when they were married and they preferred the quiet life at their farm home near Heltonville.

They had been "hitched," as country folks called it, a couple of weeks when some folks at the church they attended decided it was time for a chivaree for them. A chivaree also can be spelled charivari and is pronounced shiv'a-ree'. The dictionary says it is "a noisy mock serenade to newlyweds."

The chivaree occurred when church members forgot the 11th commandment, "Thou shalt not pester thy friends." They planned the event after a church meeting in the heat of a midsummer night when Jesse and Fern were absent.

The perpetrators of the chivaree went by caravan in autos of the 1930s and entered onto the farm lane churning up clouds of dust along the narrow gravel road.

Jesse and Fern lived about a half-mile off the road. About half the lane was on a sandstone creek bottom. The rest was on a dirt lane. If it hadn't been dark, the couple would have thought the Oklahoma dust bowl had blown in from the West.

The visitors seemed to spring from their cars in unison, clanging cans, pots and pans and pounding wash tubs, setting off skyrockets and yelling greetings of joy. This was followed by a few selections of down home music led by the church song leader.

Midway through the singing, Jesse and Fern decided the night's entertainment would not go away if ignored. A light from a kerosene lamp was turned up inside the house before Jesse, clad in bib overalls, came out looking embarrassed. Fern followed later, expressing shock and amazement, which was normal for brides at such carryings on.

Jesse allowed as to how it would be okay if the congregation decided to make itself at home. That was the signal for women to remove an assortment of precooked food from the cars. Makeshift tables were set and the noise stilled a bit while the food, cooked as only farm wives could, was consumed.

Fern and Jesse gradually grew more at ease, realizing a chivaree wasn't something that would be done for just anyone.

The crowd began to disperse as the clock neared 11 and the farmers began to think about getting up before dawn to milk. Jesse and Fern said good byes to each family.

"It'll be a long time before those two forget this night," said one farmer as he prepared to leave in his 1935 Studebaker.

Jesse and Fern were married 40 years and chances are in the quiet of a warm evening they would remember the night a hundred or so friends and neighbors wished them a lifetime of togetherness.

In years to come, the neighborliness of chivarees would end. People became more reserved, too busy, too self-centered to welcome newly-weds. And many of those just married would resent an intrusion into their lives.

Chivaree would become just a seldom-sought word in the dictionary where it remains.

Oh, Shucks

Rural residents were easy to please when it came to entertainment in the depression. Even corn husking could attract a crowd.

Farmers around Lawrence County shucked, husked some called it, into the 1940s when mechanical pickers became more numerous.

Men, even in towns, bragged how fast they could husk the ears from stalks much like they boast of their golf games today. The late James Guthrie, in his book, a *Quarter Century In*

Lawrence County (1917-1941), noted that three "city slickers" engaged in a contest in November, 1937. Educator H. H. Mourer defeated Dr. A. E. Newland and banker Ralph Moore.

That impromptu contest sparked much larger shuck-offs in October, 1938, in which 54 farmers competed in township contests. My dad was one of the entrants, which pleased me because he didn't talk much about any athletic ability or any other talent he had. I did know he could shuck two rows while my brother and I could barely keep up on a third.

I wasn't a bit happy when Mom made us go to school that brisk October morning of the township contest. We had planned to watch what was the first—and would be the last—in Pleasant Run Township. Dad wanted a cheering section but knew better than to overrule Mom.

Dad, she correctly said, had shucked corn from dawn to dusk and didn't need to be ordered to move as fast as he can and as well as his ability allowed.

Dad nodded and said, "Whoever wins is gonna do so because of effort, experience and skill. All the hootin' and hollerin' in the world won't make them ears go into the wagon any faster."

He watched us leave to catch the bus, saying, "I'll give you all the details when you get home."

We grumbled all the way to school that morning. We were even more unhappy when we learned Leonard Chambers and other sons of contestants were out at the contest site northwest of Heltonville.

My mind that morning wasn't anywhere near the fourth grade subjects teacher William Wright was trying to teach.

All I could visualize was Dad grabbing an ear of corn with his left hand, swinging the double hook on his right hand into the shucks, ripping back the husks, breaking off the ear and banging it against the backboard of the wagon.

I had shucked enough corn with Dad to know he worked smoothly and quickly, rhythmically, always leaving the ears clean. Fortunately I didn't have to wait too long to learn who won.

Buck, a school bus driver, found me on the playground. "Your pa won," he said. "Didn't have no trouble at all. Nobody was close to him. He looked like a machine out there." I knew he was exaggerating a bit, but I thanked Buck and spread the word, a bit braggingly, as quickly as I could.

I didn't concentrate on Mr. Wright's classes that afternoon any more than I did that morning. I did my chores that night without complaining.

Dad tried to bring me back to earth. He said there was more to life than winning contests and games. "Everybody is good at one thing or another. Having shucked corn for 35 years or so, I just happen to be good at that, since I've done it so much."

I didn't say much the next day or even when Dad was pictured in both the *Bedford Daily Times* and the *Bedford Daily Mail* with the other township winners.

The story listed their rewards. Each received new overalls, new shirts, new denim jackets and other items donated by Bedford merchants.

I had to stay in school again a few days later. Dad, Wesley Trogdon, competed against township winners Leland Grissom, Spice Valley; Lloyd Bodenhamer, Marshall; John Roberts, Bono; Alfred Case, Guthrie; Harry Burton, Marion; Alva Wagoner, Perry; Paul Dodd, Indian Creek, and Charles Hayes, Shawswick.

It was a major event for that time. Gov. Clifford Townsend fired a shot to start the contest, then competed against some other celebrities.

Harry Burton won the event held near Mitchell, shucking 17.47 bushels in 80 minutes. Dad was third, not too far behind.

Dad wasn't too upset, using his loss as a lesson, "Take this to heart, son. No matter how good you are at whatever it is, there will always be someone, somewhere, better than you."

It was a message that still applies to individuals, to athletes, to teams or chess or checker players.

One-Armed Bandits

More than one young man got behind the 8-ball for visiting Pete's Pool Room in Heltonville. It wasn't that parents objected to pool. Some of their adult friends were pool players.

They did, however, oppose to some of the things that went on in Pete's. And they knew everything that did go on. Almost all, that is. Had they known there were more than pool tables in the place, which was in an abandoned store down by the railroad, they would have complained even more.

It wasn't the pool tables that caused a problem. It was the "one-armed bandits," "the coin collectors," we learned to call them." They snatched our coins, clinking a few in return from time to time just to keep us dropping in more. Sooner or later a few of us would lose all our spending money, which wasn't much to start with.

The nickel machine was old, had a handle that was hard to pull and made so much noise in the back room where it was hidden that a juke box had to be played loudly out front to dull the sound.

The dime machine, though, was a thing of beauty. Almost new, it sang its own melody when each dime dropped into it. Some players said it allowed them to spend twice as much in half the time.

One teen-age player once hit the jackpot on the nickel machine, seeing more buffalo than he would see later in both the Dakotas. He envisioned himself a wise investor, took the money out to Pete and asked for a punch board. He invested the nickels in 25-cent punches until they disappeared.

That loser likely didn't complain when one of the slot machines mysteriously disappeared one night after Pete closed. A day or two later a small item at the bottom of Page One of the *Bedford Times-Mail* reported a nickel slot machine had been found on a county road. It had been battered open, the money taken.

A couple of days later, a teen drove into town in a Model A Ford he owned. The car had four new tires and a shiny radiator

ornament that looked like something you'd see in a Spiegel cata-
logue.

The kid said he had suddenly come onto some money.

"Yeah, yeah," a few friends said in unison, adding, "Like a lot
of nickels and dimes?" The driver just smiled, walked over to the
car, playfully kicked one of the new tires, got in, set the spark and
said:

"Be seein' ya."

He may have been completely innocent. We never knew. But
we did learn at Pete's Place that it is better to work for money
than gamble for it.

The knowledge would serve us well when the pursuit of reve-
nue led the state of Indiana to allow riverboat casinos, lotteries
and scratch off tickets in the 1990s.

With The Grain

Grain elevators were a hub of activity for men—and boys—in
rural areas. Males congregated at those places like they did at
barber shops and general stores, swapping stories and gossip,
comforting the distressed, razzing those more fortunate.

Elevators, feed mills some called them, later became busi-
nesses vastly different from Jerry Jones' feed mill on the banks of
Leatherwood Creek.

Jones, quiet and pleasant, operated the mill in Heltonville in
the 1930s and 1940s, as much, it appeared, as a convenience for
farmers as he did for a livelihood.

He was in business to serve the public. He did it by being fair,
cooperative and helpful. No one was ever known to leave the elevator with a scowl on his face. Doing business with Jerry was a
pleasant experience.

Jerry's elevator wasn't huge by 2000 standards, did not need
to be for the small farms on the hillsides of Eastern Lawrence
County.

There were few big semis around the mill. Tractors or teams
of mules or horses hitched to wagons were more numerous. Some
held grain to be sold or ground into livestock feed. At times some

contained newly-threshed wheat to be ground into flour. That grain was ground into flour and bagged by Jerry, whose clothes often were white from the dust.

Farm wives claimed the flour was the best that could be had. Their husbands contended there was no better feed for milk cows than the bran residue from the wheat.

Farmers often traded Jerry flour for the grinding bill. If they needed cash they could sell grain to Jerry, who kept the daily market price of corn and wheat posted on a chalk board so there would be no haggling over the price.

Once the flour had been ground or the grain sold, the farmer would follow Jones into a small office where he calculated the account due or payable on a 3-by-5 inch page of a booklet.

Time and progress, if it could be called that, took their toll on Jerry and his mill. Better roads, new equipment and bigger farm operations made visits by farmers less frequent.

Many farmers bought trucks and hauled their grain to big elevators in Medora and Brownstown. Some acquired their own feed grinders and, as the years passed, farm wives bought flour at stores in supermarkets.

Jerry grew older and sold the mill to new owners, who operated it for a few years. No one complained, but the mill wasn't the same without Jerry.

The mill no longer stands. But no visitor ever forgot the place or Jerry Jones, a businessman who took time to be nice to people.

Garage Guru

Abe Martin was a mechanic, not Kin Hubbard's "Abe Martin," who espoused the rustic cracker barrel philosophy of Indiana's Brown County.

This Abe was real, a philosopher who could entertain a visitor and irritate a customer.

Many of his visitors came for enjoyment. Others came in autos in need of engine repair or on tractors that needed tune-ups. Abe was good at repairs. He was better at conversations and putting off today what could be done better tomorrow at his small shop.

He listened as each customer arrived at his small garage east of Heltonville on Ind. 58, made a few suggestions, then replied, no matter the problem, "I'll get right on it."

"Right on it," was a relative term.

In a day or two, the owner would return to hear Abe explain, "Haven't had time to get it back together, but I'll get right on it."

When a car, gasoline washing machine engine or tractor owner looked inside the garage he wondered if the repairs would ever be made. The floor was dirt, but gallons of thick oil that had soaked into the earth made it as hard as concrete. Tractor parts were scattered amid rings and pistons and distributor wires from cars. An engine block from a truck swung on a chain from a beam under the roof.

It was taken for granted that somehow, some way Abe would get the right part back in the right engine.

It might take three, four or more visits to Abe's place before the repairs were made. Regular customers learned no work would be done before its time, that time being when Abe was good and ready to do it. They just kept coming back to let Abe know he was important in their lives.

And he did the work at reasonable prices. When a customer asked the cost of his service, Abe would hem and haw and suggest, a little embarrassed, "Oh, how does $5 sound." Most customers, who knew the value of a job well done, often paid him more, pulling $8, sometimes $10, from worn wallets.

"Much obliged," Abe said, his ever-present grin a bit broader. If a customer mentioned he also had a tractor that needed fixed, Abe invariably would nod and add, "Bring it in. I'll get right on it."

Other work needed to be done, but Abe would wait to get "right on it." He would instead open a soft drink from a small cooler, flip off the water, and resume his conversation with his guests.

Work could be done anytime. Friendship could not wait.

Forging Friendship

Blacksmith shops also were a diversion from the routine, none more so than Jim East's place in Heltonville. Jim was as kind as Abe Martin, but a bit more conscientious.

His house was next door to his shop, but he spent more time in his workplace. He needed to in order to get his work done when promised.

Jim was tall and thin, but his hands were large and sinewy and his brawny arms carried iron-tight muscles. But his voice was as soft as tin and his speech as refined as a minister's.

March was his busiest month. Farmers, eager to get into the fields, came to Jim to have their horses shod, plow points sharpened, tools repaired, clevises and hooks fashioned.

We could watch Jim work around an anvil, a forge with bellows, a tub of water, blackened and rusty pieces of iron, a pile of coal, tools of all shapes and sizes, hammers, tongs, grips and snips.

Jim seemed to do five things at once and still carry on a conversation. He moved slowly, but purposefully, sometimes rubbing his hands on his rubber apron before adjusting his wire rim glasses for a closer look at what he was doing.

He let us turn a crank that operated a fan which forced air into the coal to feed the fire in the forge. The coal had the smell of sulphur as the heat turned the metal red, then white, allowing Jim to pound it into whatever shape he wanted. Once that was done, he dropped the metal into a tub of water that popped and sizzled as it cooled the iron.

It was in the forge and at the anvil that Jim shaped new points for plow shares and fitted shoes for horses and bent iron for whatever purposes it was needed.

It was not unusual for a farmer to say, "Don't know what we'd do without you, Jim."

Jim wasn't so certain. "I can see the day coming when blacksmiths won't be all that important," he admitted. "Machinery is getting bigger and better. Tractors have about replaced horses and farmers can buy factory-built parts that can be replaced cheaper than I can repair them."

He was thoughtful enough to tell a pre-teen, "I don't have too many good years left anyhow." It was allaying our concern for his welfare.

His forecast was right. Blacksmith shops slowly vanished and only a few remain in the nation's small towns.

Doctor Plus

Jasper Cain was a rural family doctor by profession. He was a friend, adviser, confidant, farmer, hunter, humanitarian by choice. He also was a font of information and enjoyment.

And he cared about the people around him. He cared so much he forgot at times his own welfare and comfort. He remained a doctor when it would have been easier to do all the other things he enjoyed.

"Doc" did not confine his practice to his tiny office in Heltonville. He ranged for miles through the hills and hollows in the 1920s and 1930s, sometimes in the early 1940s, doing what he could to cure his patients.

He often had to wait to be paid, but he didn't fret about it. He knew most people would pay him whenever they could.

"Doc" never seemed to get satisfaction from making money. Other things thrilled him more than bank deposits. He didn't make much money for serving two terms as Pleasant Run Township trustee, but he thought he was doing something worthwhile by seeing the school was run properly.

"Doc" seemed happiest when he was on the land, farming, hunting, walking, watching the wildlife.

Some of his best times came on hot summer days when he joined his son, Ed, as he custom combined wheat for farmers with an Allis Chalmers tractor that pulled an Allis Chalmers combine. When the rig reached our fields, "Doc" perched himself on the back of a wagon, lighted a cigar, made sure the match was snuffed and treated me—an early teen—as an adult.

Whatever "Doc" said was worthwhile. There were no X-rated remarks. He talked about the war in the Pacific and in Europe, about rationing, about his life as a country doctor, about the people of the community.

When Ed unloaded the hopper into burlap bags, "Doc" helped hold the sacks as the grain augured into them. Once finished, he taught me slowly, clearly, patiently, how to tie a miller's knot.

He laughed as he watched me chase rabbits that had leaped from the wheat as the combine neared. When one rabbit lost a leg in the cutting blade, he gently tied cloth on the wound, eased the animal to the ground, watched it tremble in fright, then flee as best as it could on three legs.

"Doc" was without pretense. He was, late in life, hunting with another friend when some birds flew over. He aimed his shotgun and one of the birds plummeted to earth near their boats.

"Good shot, Doc," his companion said. Doc just smiled.

That afternoon as he left his friend, he confessed, "There's something you ought to know. I wasn't shooting at the bird I hit. I was aiming at one off to the left."

The friend said, "You didn't have to tell me that, 'Doc.' "

Doc grinned and said, "I feel better for doing it, though."

He was the last doctor to practice in Heltonville. The "Doc" Cains are gone from small, unincorporated towns and patients drive to medical centers for care that is more hurried and impersonal.

Roadhouses

Southern Indiana roadhouses of the 1930s and 1940s, like many so-called "dins of inequities," weren't as bad as their reputations.

Many adults criticized them. So did preachers. To mothers they were places where the booze flowed freely, the dancing was wild and the combination of each activity led to lascivious and lecherous behavior.

To the men and women who visited the nightspots, they were places for fun and relaxation in a time when the nation was creeping out of the long depression, places where you could kick off your shoes and dance to the mellow music of musicians from nearby towns.

As teens we heard those vastly different versions about Shady Springs and Maple Leaf on U.S. 50 east of Bedford and Tarry Park and the Green Lantern off Ind. 37 between Bedford and Mitchell.

A few of the places still operated into the mid-1940s. I was 15 when two older, more curious teens, convinced me to accompany them to Shady Springs. I was as green as a gourd, three years from needing a razor and as scared as a rabbit in hunting season.

"Just act like you own the place," one of them said. "Sure," I thought. I looked more 13 than 18, the age of admittance, and shook with fear when a man inside the door took our admission fee and said, "Hold out your hand."

"Huh?" I asked.

"Need to stamp your hand so you can come and go the rest of the night," he said. It was obvious age wasn't a criteria for admittance, at least to that doorkeeper.

The place was packed, dimly-lit, the air filled with cigarette smoke that floated like clouds against the low ceiling. No one seemed to mind.

Couples were there. So were women in search of men and men looking for women. We were there out of curiosity and, as we told ourselves, to do research for other teens.

"Need a set up?" a waitress asked. I was about to tell her I could not sit up any straighter than my 5 feet 6 body would allow when a companion quickly offset my ignorance, ordering a Coke and a bucket of ice.

We watched as a couple at the next table spiked their "set ups" with liquor poured from bottles kept under the table lest a lawman decided to snoop around.

We soon eased our way through the tables and left unseen by anyone we knew. As naive as we were, we still wondered what made such places as attractive as we heard or as evil as others said.

Never did it dawn on us that those little cabins on some of the roadhouse grounds were not only being used as lodging for motorists but for amorous couples with more than travel on their minds. One joke of the time went like this:

Customer: "How much is a cabin for the night?"

Operator: "Let me think. I'm not sure I've ever rented one for that long."

We learned later that Tarry Park on Ind. 37 south of Bedford was one of more popular—and most respected—night spots of the area. It featured some of the best musicians around, including groups from Bloomington who refused to play at places with more rowdy crowds. Except for occasional breaks, the musicians sometimes played until the sun began to rise, or so we were told.

When the liquor flasks ran dry, the guests drank soft drinks and ate sandwiches and listened to the sounds of the songs of vocalists like Gib Harris of Bloomington.

Most of the roadhouses and dance halls closed before the 1940s ended and entertainment shifted to other venues.

*   *   *

The tourists cabins on U.S. 50 near the community of Fairview were fronted by an office and general store but had no roadhouse on the grounds. It did have a slot machine where more than one teen learned that gambling was a poor investment of hard earned coins.

Fishing Tale

Fishing and hunting were more necessities than sports in the 1930s. They were sources of food for families who lived in small towns or on lots without farm fields.

They could still be the source of fun and stories to regale friends. Among the more humorous came from two men who were fishing in a small lake above a dam east of Heltonville.

All went well until a game warden left his car on the road and headed toward the dam. One of the men, dropping his fishing pole, fled in the opposite direction, cutting through briers and trees, ignoring scratches and cuts.

Exhausted, he paused for breath and waited for the pursuing warden, who, between gasps, demanded to see his fishing license. The man pulled a valid license from his wallet.

"Man, why did you run like that if you had a license?" the warden asked.

Still panting, the man answered, "Cause my buddy back there at the dam didn't have one and you'll never catch him now."

He was right. His friend had fled the scene and was nowhere to be seen. Even the game warden was said to have laughed as they walked toward the road.

Barbershop Banter

Men, young and old, could be regaled at barber shops in Heltonville, Norman and other small towns. Barbers served grizzled outdoorsmen who spun yarns for their young sons to record in memory vaults to be replayed later.

Rural women seldom visited beauty salons for there were none in rural areas at the time. They cut each other's hair. Their permanents were shaped by ingredients from a bottle and applied by a relative or neighbor.

Girls primped for dates by shaping their hair with curlers heated over the kerosene lamp shade or a kitchen range. The smell of singed hair meant a coiffure was being shaped for a Saturday night date.

Residents of homes without indoor plumbing bathed in metal wash tubs filled with heated water from a spring or a well, often hand dug. They were more ritual than fun.

Amusement came at the barber shops where grooming was just one of the attractions. The customers swapped stories, more true than false for real life at the time was more exciting than fiction.

Men, their whiskers a week old, were shaved by barbers, who honed straight razors on a whetstone and stropped them on a strip of leather that hung from the chair. Hardened men mumbled, through hot towels, that they were being scalded as their beards were being softened. The barber, busy creating shaving foam from soap in a mug, paid them no heed.

We boys learned to keep quiet, being no match for men who had spent decades telling stories, learning to spice their conversations with descriptive terms seldom used in today's more dignified speech.

Men still swap stories, but not the way they did a half-century ago. The color has faded from conversations. Story tellers now sound like TV commentators. They watch their grammar, punctuate their phrases and choose their words like they were in Dale Carnage speech classes.

The result is language that's deader than a door nail, flatter than a fritter, as dull as dishwater.

That would be expected from what our elders called "highfalutin, would-be muckety-mucks interested in puttin' on the dog and makin' folks think the sun rises to hear them crow."

We harken back decades to a time when farmers around Heltonville spiced their language with realism. They stole phrases from others, coined their own and mixed them into sentences that told stories as expressively and colorfully as pictures of the autumn landscape.

They didn't just feel well or poorly. They felt tolerably well, downright puny, had no gumption or get-up-and-go and would have to get better to die.

If they showed up at the barber shop down-in-the-mouth, the "razor stropper" told them they looked like they'd been "rode hard and put away wet."

No one entered the shop to get his "ears set out" without a customer telling the others, "Look at what the cat drug in." Anyone who protested was told not to have a "conniption fit."

The men had their own view of the opposite sex. Some women were as "purty as pictures," as "cute as ponies in pig lots" or as "sweet as maple sugar."

Some, the men, said, had faces that could stop newly-wound seven-day clocks. Some were as ugly as mud fences. A few were as homely as lye soap.

If a less-than-pretty woman walked by, someone would observe, "She can't help being ugly, but she could stay home." A man with muscles like rocks would be stronger than an ox, could go bear hunting with a switch or scare the bejabbers out of a stranger.

Youngsters who did cartwheels and somersaults on the grass across the road flopped around like chickens with their heads cut off.

Some baseball or basketball players were faster than greased lightning. Others were as sluggish as sorghum in January, as slow as February, or so pokey bread crumbs wouldn't fall off their laps when they walked. A few were as awkward a pregnant sow on ice.

Some boys were as sharp as tacks, a few had minds as quick as steel traps, some had brains but no horse sense.

Not all kids were smart. Some were "as green as gourds." If some had a brain it would die of loneliness. Boys who were naive looked like they had just fallen off a hay wagon on the road to nowhere.

A ne'er-do-well wasn't worth the salt that went into his bread. A scoundrel wasn't worth the powder it would take to blow him off a rail fence.

Now and then a farmer would complain he was too poor to pay attention, let alone his taxes. The truth was, almost all of them were actually happier than hogs in slop.

Some of the men lived high on the hog, but others claimed they were so poor they ate one day and swallowed the next.

None of the men spent too much time in the barber shop, or anywhere else, lest they plant their feet in concrete or get set in their ways. Besides, they were all busier than bees in bras or one-armed paper hangers at house cleaning time. There was so much work to do they didn't even have time to cuss the cat.

They needed time to be alone. After all, it took a heap of thinkin' to conjure up a new sayin' that would bring tears to a glass eye.

Some had dogs that wouldn't hunt, which meant they weren't worth much except to scratch fleas. Others told them to stay positive because, "raccoon eyes don't shine down on the same dog every day."

Once they had exhaused the "sayings," as they called such phrases, the men argued about whatever came to mind. "Baseball players were overpaid. Joe DiMaggio had signed a contract for $80,000 a year. Gene Autry is making $100,000 a year. Too much for riding a horse, pluckin' a guitar and singin' western songs."

A Gene Autry fan would object. "Yeah, but that includes incentive pay for kissing his horse Champion." Little did the men realize that athletes would eventually ink $80 million contracts or that actors would make millions for appearing in inane television shows.

Newspapers

Newspapers were both a source of entertainment and humor as well as news in the 1930s and 1940s.

Comic strips thrilled youngsters, adults related to Dorothy Dix and her advise columns. Sports pages covered baseball in the summer, football in the fall and basketball in the winter. Columnists sometimes traded barbs with those on other papers.

News was personalized. Stories were about people subscribers knew. "Items," as they were called, let readers know who called on what neighbor, had stories relevant to their lives and comics that were humorous, not political statements.

The comics pages featured "Board and Room" with "The Judge" and his buddy "Emerson" who were always good for laughs. "Dixie Dugan" was young and single, but a bit too old for teen-agers. "Mickey Finn" was a role model as big city police detective who usually nabbed the culprit. "Big Chief Wahoo" gave insight into Indian culture. "Popeye" ate spinach, wooed "Olive Oyl" and tormented pal "Wimpy," who could eat hamburgers faster than they could be fried at Alfred's Restaurant in Bedford.

"Buck Rogers, 25th Century AD," looked five centuries into a fictional future that the reality of technology would precede by more than four centuries.

"Joe Palooka," a world champion boxer, took on foes in fiction while Joe Louis kayoed in reality any "bum of the month" contender who dared face him.

Newspapers at that time had little competition. Few small towns had radio stations. Television was years away. What rivalry existed was between publishers. Many county seats had two newspapers, one that leaned Republican, the other Democrat. Some carried political labels and did not use subterfuge to confuse readers.

Residents of Lawrence County could choose between the *Bedford Daily Times* and the *Bedford Daily Mail*.

Republicans preferred the *Daily Mail*, said its word was as dependable as the Bible. Democrats liked the *Daily Times*, because it ridiculed Republicans. Newsmakers liked both since they usually were mentioned in each paper. So did athletes and coaches.

A friend's parents took both papers, which he said made evenings exiting. "Dad sits on one side the Aladdin's coal oil lamp and reads the *Daily Mail*. Mom sits on the other side, knits awhile, then reads the *Daily Times*.

"Dad always finds some anti-Democrat item and reads it out loud to Mom. She gets upset until she finds a story that makes the Republicans look bad, reads it to him and adds, 'So take that.'

"Dad then winks at me so I'll know the spats won't lead to divorce."

That choice of newspapers ended on Saturday, February 10, 1942. Instead of two papers, Bedford would have one—as it still does—the merged *Bedford-Times Mail*. Few partisans were pleased.

A teacher dramatized the merger the following Monday. "*The Times*," she said, "had praised every Democrat and vilified each Republican who was in office or sought to be." The *Daily Mail*, she added, was "surly, even vicious, toward Democrats. I remember when it printed—right on the first page—every morsel of dirt it could find about Paul McNutt when he was governor."

When she hesitated, a student asked, "Which paper did you like best?"

She turned red, said, wisely, "The word is better not best," and added, "I think it's time we turn to our lesson for today."

The merger of the two Bedford newspapers was part of a trend that continued through the century. Corporations now run newspaper chains like McDonald's restaurants, one almost a duplicate of another. Readers must subscribe to out-of-town newspapers or news magazines to find diverse opinions.

And too often our thinking, our votes and the way we cast our ballots are shaped by what we read and by television with its opinionated talk shows and abbreviated newscasts, often slanted in content.

Magazines

Magazines were sources of information and entertainment but most catered then, as now, to the opinions and beliefs of their managers.

The *Saturday Evening Post* was popular among rural and small town subscribers. Its Norman Rockwell covers illustrated the America of the 1930s and 1940s and a desire to retain traditional values in the midst of depression. Despite its name it arrived on Thursday or Friday to be read over weekends.

Its stories were written for common folks who sought sunlight among darkness. Short stories were about fictional characters that were relevant; cartoons were laughable without being crude. It was a family magazine as wholesome for a pre-teen as for an adult. It was, as it had been for decades, enjoyable reading for middle-class America. Its editorial matter addressed issues that affected readers both rich and poor. But it was not, as no publication ever is, free of criticism.

Critics said *The Post* changed from entertainment and enlightenment into a weapon of political warfare against President Roosevelt. That conservatism, they claimed, caused "a decline in content and style causing a decline in prestige and authority."

Those critics said its "conservative viewpoint and admiration for material success" appealed to millions and "set out to interpret America" as it saw it. Liberals were difficult to please then as now. They preferred the highbrow *New Yorker*, urbane and sophisticated, with humor and content that had little meaning for the few readers in heartland America who saw it in the pre-war years.

As was *Vanity Fair*, the *New Yorker* was written for the elite by the elite, not for the masses as were the *Saturday Evening Post* and *Colliers*, another popular publication. Average Americans were not yet ready for news of the arts, architecture or aristocracy.

Farm magazines like *Farm Journal* and *Country Gentleman*, were popular in the Midwest and the *Farmer's Guide* was a must for many Hoosiers. *The Grit*, a weekly magazine that sold for a dime, as I recall, was a magazine-like publication printed in a tabloid newspaper format. Its stories were off-beat, often interesting and sometimes believable.

Children—and some grownups- enjoyed "Superman" and "Captain Marvel" and other comic books.

Music Machines

Few of us had an appreciation for good music, but most of us enjoyed tunes sometimes played on guitars and banjoes by self-taught neighbors.

Our Victrola was an RCA Victor, a company that had taken over the Victor Talking Machine Company in 1929. That "music machine," as we called it, had a crank at the side that hand-wound a spring-powered motor that spun the turntable which held only one record at a time.

The slots in the cabinet for the 78 records were usually bare, our library of discs usually limited to three or four. I recall only "The Trail of the Lonesome Pine" record that we played over and over.

In time, the Victrolas lost out to the louder and more flexible electronic combination systems. Only cheap portables and children's phonographs continued to utilize acoustic reproduction.

Our player piano had a far different sound. Songs were on rolls, the paper punched with holes to create the music. I was too young to grasp its operation, but a source explained: "Power was generated by the operation of two foot pedals, while the music was represented by the perforations on the interchangeable rolls of paper. Tones could be changed by altering the force on the foot pedals."

A skilled operator, it is said, could produce songs that appeared to be solo performances despite the rolls that played. The player piano could be operated by hand as was a regular piano, but no one in our family was adept at the keyboard.

An older sister's date often sat down to play while she primped. He was still playing at 10 p.m. to her disgust, ending her hopes for a night out. A youth in those days was happy for a cheap date even if he had to wait for a week to be forgiven.

Sugar Lickin' Good

The good times came for Grandma J. after the work was done at the sugar house. The sap had been boiled into syrup and poured into pails. Most of it would be sold to customers from town, who would soon come, each to buy a gallon, maybe more.

The rest wasn't for sale. Not at any price. It was Mrs. J.'s personal stock, and it would be used to bring smiles to her grandchildren, who came each weekend to find treats no general store carried.

Mrs. J. was stooped at the shoulders and her silver hair was pulled back into a bun. She looked older than she was. Years of hard work on the farm near Heltonville had done that to her.

Her hands shook, letting the teacup chatter against the saucer when she carried her coffee to the table to sit for brief spells on busy mornings. An apron covered the home-sewn print dresses she wore, giving her a place to rub the palms of her hands as she worked in the kitchen. A big smile covered her face, hiding six decades of hardship.

We, her grandchildren, hadn't yet been told about her being widowed young and raising alone her children, who were our mothers. She was remarried briefly, but that didn't interest us as much as the happiness she gave us.

Any Saturday morning was a delight. By the time we arrived she had baked a half-dozen pies, a big flat chocolate cake on a 30 by 30 inch tin and a devil's food or angel food cake.

March was even a better time to visit. She waited until we showed up on Saturday morning to pry the lid off a pail, pour some of the syrup into a pan, then heat it over the wood stove.

She beat the warm syrup and poured it into a into a pan divided into cups to cool outdoors. It would take some time for the syrup to harden, but the wait would be worth it. Meantime, there were magazines like *Collier's*, *Saturday Evening Post*, *Country Gentleman*, *Capper's Farmer* and *Farm Journal* to read.

She later brought in the pan, turned it upside down and banged it against the table top. The sugar cakes fell out, round and unbroken, our special treats.

We ate slowly, savoring each nibble, extending the preciousness of the moment. Grandma sometimes handed each of us visitors two more cakes as we left.

When I took one to school later, three or four friends bartered for it, offering me candy bars or whatever they had of worth. I turned down each offer. They had the last laugh, though.

When I told Grandma about it the next Saturday, she broke one of the sugar cakes into quarters, wrapped them in wax paper and handed them to me, saying, gently, "Take these to school Monday. And learn to share with others what joy you get in life."

*   *   *

I learned Grandma had died when I returned to the barracks after a day in basic training at Camp Breckenridge in the winter of 1951-1952.

The captain had a three-day pass ready. I was a recruit, but he drove me out to the state highway from where I hitchhiked home.

Those Saturday mornings spent with her a decade earlier were a companion on the way home.

Different Treat

Ben didn't serve sugar cakes or chocolate pies on Saturdays in winter but he did dish out philosphy and wisdom. He was at peace with his environment, having learned over 60-plus years that life is a series of peaks and valleys. Good, he knew, usually followed bad.

Ben had spent his adult life on a little farm east of Heltonville. working with a team of horses after most of his neighbors had bought powerful Farmall, John Deere and Allis-Chalmers tractors.

There was no point, he reasoned, to adapt to the new. The shadows were lengthening on his life and his days were too short to spend learning new ways. He kept busy, though, working and thinking, often doing both at the same time.

One of those times came on a mid-winter Saturday about 1940 when the temperature was in the single digits. He had hitched his horses to a sled and used it to bring two shocks of fodder from the snow-covered corn field to the barn.

He tugged the shocks into the gangway, then unhitched and unharnessed the team. It did not bother him when a neighbor stopped by as he fed the team. Horses, he often said, understood him better than most people.

Ear-flaps dangled from Ben's cap. He wore a denim jacket over overalls and a flannel shirt. His yellow and gray gloves had double thumbs so they could be worn on either hand. A buckle was missing from each of his high-top overshoes.

Ben nodded, friendly-like, when he turned and saw the neighbor lad who had arrived for a visit. "Fixin' to shuck the corn," he said, nodding toward the stalks in the barn. "You might just as well sit and gab with me while I work. His visitor was an 11-year-old neighbor, but Ben made him feel like an adult.

Ben fitted a shucking hook over the glove on his right hand, stooped down on his knees and started husking the ears from the stalks. He flipped each ear toward a feed bin, seldom making an errant toss. He stopped once, holding a big ear in one hand, a nubbin in the other.

"These two ears are like life," he said. "Some things turn out well, others not so good."

One of the horses snorted, emitting a cloud of steam. A cow mooed softly. The boy eyed the two ears and nodded to acknowledge he understood. He hunkered down into his jacket against the cold and said, "Seems like a long time until spring."

Ben looked up, stopped for a moment, and replied, "Don't rush through life, son. Enjoy each minute you can. Winter ain't all that bad. It's a time to rest up from the year that's done past and get ready for the year that's a-comin'."

His visitor waited. Ben went on, "Just think of it as half -time of a basketball game. It's a time to stop and take a look at where you've been and where you're headed."

"Sort of like a recess at school, huh?" the boy asked.

Ben nodded and continued to separate the corn from the stalks. When he finished, he carried some of the fodder to the mangers in the barn. The animals wasted no time sampling it.

The boy tugged the collar of his coat around his neck and pulled the sock cap over his ears. "Guess I'd better be headin' home," he said. He walked to the big doors at the end of the barn, then ambled back to where Ben was. "I reckon the cold winter weather will make us enjoy spring more," he said.

Ben nodded. A grin crept across his wrinkled face, lined like a road map. It had been a morning well spent. He could have done the work anytime. An opportunity to share his knowledge with a youngster was rare.

*   *   *

There were other men, with old-time names like Clyde, Roy, Sam, Oval, Clarence and George, who shared their reservoirs of knowledge. All have long since passed on to their rewards. All were fountains of advice and, like Ben, were as colorful as the redbud and dogwood of spring and the leaves of autumn along the roads of our lives.

AMERICANS ALL

"Folks Like Us"

Our childhood world was one dimensional. It was white, Protestant, rural in character and of northern European heritage. If life was a boat, we were all in it together.

The only arguments I heard were over politics, almost all angry words between neighbors laced with softening humor. We were of one culture and many of us were related, however distantly.

I must have been eight or nine before I talked to a black person for the first time. I knew Dad had spoken well of a few he knew in Bedford but there were none in our neighborhood and none in our school.

That must have been why Dad mentioned one Saturday morning, "There's something you ought to know before we start cuttin' wood and clearin' brush this morning."

I was curious, but he explained: "We're gonna trade some help."

"So what?" I wondered. "We've swapped help before with Sam, Elmer, George, Wilmer, Clyde and a lot of other farmers around here."

He nodded, but added, "This help, a man from Bedford, a mighty fine one, is black." We are going to clean some trees and brush from that little hollow that reaches up into the field over by Clarence Harrell's. And "Mr. Brown," I think he called him, "is going to take home a load of wood for helping us."

En route to the work site he explained that not everyone liked to work with blacks or anyone else who isn't white like we were.

Mr. Brown was not alone either when he arrived in a small pickup truck. His son, Willie, about my age, was with him.

The two of us piled limbs and brush our fathers cut, but we didn't talk much at first. The icy reserve that separated us thawed gradually like the once frozen dirt and we traded stories about our schools and our interests.

Meantime Dad and Mr. Brown were at opposite ends of a crosscut saw, working in harmony to cut small trees and saplings into sticks of wood, the number growing by the minute.

When they stopped to drink coffee from a Thermos, Willie and me ran home for cocoa and cookies. The morning passed quickly and by noon "Mr. Brown" had loaded his truck.

Dad told him to let us know when he needed another load. "Be seeing you," Willie said, returning our wave.

As we walked home I told Dad, "They seem the same as folks like us."

He picked up his tools and said, "That may be the wisest lesson thing you've learned this week."

Racial Bias

Two years later we were in Upper Marlboro, Maryland, visiting a sister and her husband, who worked in nearby Washington, D. C. Their house was small and I sought space by spending time across the road at a tobacco sale barn.

Leaf of tobacco plants, grown by farmers in the area, hung from rafters where it was auctioned to cigarette companies. It was an expansive building where we were free to roam and ask questions answered by men, both black and white.

Within a day or two I had made friends with a black my age, who was as curious about me as I was about him. We learned about each other's interests and shared our limited experiences. Our races were never mentioned.

When a Friday came, I mentioned my brother and I planned to attend a movie at the theater a few blocks away. "You want to sit with us?" I asked naively.

"I can't do that," he said, a hint of disappointment in his voice. But he did not explain.

The reason was apparent at the theater that night. Blacks were relegated to a balcony. Only whites were seated on the main level. The unfairness of that was obvious to even a pre-teen with limited experiences. It was our introduction into segregated America, a nation that was not equal under God.

Without Prejudice

It also was about that time I learned there was more than the one church, the one religion, I had known.

I had permission to spend a Friday evening before the basketball game with Jackie Lantz, a classmate who lived across Ind. 58 from the school. Supper, unusual for a farm youth, was built around eggs served without meat. It was of no matter, eggs were a favorite food and the meal was good and filling.

When I told Mom later, she explained the Lantz family was Catholic, which meant it did not eat meat on Fridays. "Can I still be friends with Jackie?" I asked.

She laughed. "Sure," she said, "and with any Jews, Lutherans, Greeks, Jehovah Witnesses, Mormons or any other faith who wants to be your friend in return.

Bad Calls

It was mostly curiosity that led us to drive from Heltonville to a basketball game at Clearspring that Saturday night in the winter of 1947-48.

Oh, we were friends with the Cummings boys, Dan Bowman other players on the Clearspring High School team. But we could see them in action any night that Heltonville didn't have a game.

It was Crispus Attucks, the opposing team, that made us curious. It was a segregated school, its players all black. We had played in and watched basketball games for years, but had seen few black players, certainly no all-black teams.

Refused to be scheduled by central Indiana schools, the Attucks team had driven the 60 or so miles to Clearspring on a bad night in winter to play. The travel was not unusual. Their schedule included teams from small towns like Windfall, Freetown and Vallonia.

Unlike most big city schools, Crispus Attucks had no fancy warm up suits, just pants and jerseys that looked like underwear vests, faded green with small numbers that were hard to read.

The players went through a fancy pregame routine that made the usual drills seem dull. A victory over the hometown Warriors appeared certain.

Attucks' coach was Fitzhugh Lyons; his big scorers League Bailey and Everett Overton. They and the rest of the team had learned to expect no break from "homers," which referees hired by host schools were called.

Clearspring led 20-17 at the half and it was obvious any questionable calls had gone to the home team. Fitzhugh Lyons expected that, after years on the road with his Tigers. But neither he nor we four visitors from Heltonville expected what happened in the second half. Attucks tied the score at 20-20, then four more times before Clearspring won 45-53.

The officiating had made that possible. The calls weren't just questionable. They were obviously biased. Coach Lyons walked off the floor, stopped at a brick wall and pounded his fists in frustration.

"You never get used to being cheated," a friend said. Even some Clearspring fan agreed "home cookin" had made the difference. Attucks had scored two more field goals, but Clearspring had an 11-5 edge in free throws thanks to personal fouls called against Attucks players.

Lyons was still fuming as he followed his players to the cars that would take them home. If it was a normal trip, there would be no restaurant that would allow them to stop for food.

Postscript: A few years late Crispus Attucks became a power in Indiana high school basketball, winning state championships in 1955, 1956 and 1959. Crispus Attucks later became a middle school.

After one of my newspaper columns mentioned the game, Mrs. Lyons wrote to say she was certain the stress of continual travel to games and the unfair officiating led to the pre-mature death of her husband.

*   *   *

It would not be until the 1950s and 1960s that peaceful demonstrations and civil rights legislation helped deter some of the obvious bias against blacks and other minorities. But personal prejudices remain as they have since the start of mankind.

FARM LIFE

Men and Boys

It was the nature of their environment that caused a special bond to develop between farm boys and their fathers.

It was a relationship few urban youngsters and their dads could match, or understand. It was a companionship that started almost as soon as a boy was able to toddle out into the barn lot, his hand clutched safely to his father's.

The bond grew as the boy did, a link that strengthened as his muscles did, toughening to survive inevitable disagreements that were bound to arise as he grew older and worked side-by-side with his father from daybreak to dusk.

Life on farms in southern Indiana in the 1930s and 1940s was a continuing education, both for fathers and sons. Farm life was personal, much of the work was done by hand and many jobs required at least two people to complete.

For the fathers, it was an education in how fast a son could learn when given patient guidance. For the sons, it was an education in how much wisdom a father possessed.

It was like that for each of us in our neighborhood as it was for pre-teens in other areas. We worked at the barn, in the fields, in the woods and along the fences with our fathers while our sisters formed the same kind of closeness with their mothers.

There was a lesson, often a moral, to be learned from each chore fathers and sons did. And the chores were many and varied.

146

The sons learned how to dig post holes on the sides of rocky hills, to tamp the locust posts tight, to stretch barbed and woven wire fences that would last a generation despite the rugged terrain over which they were built. We learned if we built a good fence on our half of the dividing line, so would the farmer who took care of the other half.

We learned to mow fence rows with scythes, chop sprouts from new ground fields and to prove to others we cared about the places we lived, to contour fields to save the soil from erosion, to tend to livestock sometimes unable to care for itself.

We learned how to milk cows and separate the cream, which like most good things has a way of always coming to the top. We learned how to sow and how to reap and the time to do each. We learned how to shock wheat and cut fodder and fill silos and store fruits and vegetables.

And our fathers were always with us.

They were there to teach us the beauty of nature and the things that lived on the land, where to find mushrooms and papaws and hickory nuts and wild strawberries. And how to make extra money by showing us where to dig ginseng and other roots and where to find a buyer for them.

We learned how to saw trees and build barns and corn cribs from the lumber the trees yielded. We learned how to repair machinery or take it to a blacksmith if we couldn't fix it. We learned that few problems were insurmountable, given some thought. And we learned about life off the farm, tagging along when our fathers went to the feed mill in Heltonville, the grain elevator at Medora, the sawmill in Norman.

We went to the bank in Bedford where we watched our dads obtain loans needed to plant crops in the spring. We saw the same loans repaid when the crops were harvested in the fall.

We learned the value of credit and honesty and what was meant when someone said, "His word is as good as his bond." It made each of us feel good when the comment was about our fathers.

But nothing made us feel better than when someone compared us to our fathers.

Like most fathers, Dad didn't have grandiose plans for us, didn't sketch a blueprint for our futures. He just asked us to do whatever we chose to do as well as we could, earn what we got from life and never do anything we didn't want our mother to learn about.

Horse Sense

Mechanization came slowly to small farms in southern Indiana where many fields were on slopes or in narrow bands between hills and streams.

Teams of horses continued to pull plows, planters, cultivators, binders, mowers and wagons into the 1930s. Some farmers were reluctant to farm with tractors, others had no money to buy new equipment until the depression ended.

Horses ran on oats, corn and hay that was readily available. Tractors required gasoline, oil and storage. Some broke down in the midst of their greatest need, some were on steel wheels with four-inch lugs that banned them from paved roads. Horses always started at the tap of a rein.

Men who depended on horses for farm work treated them well. I sometimes thought Dad liked his team of sorrels better than me. He treated them with sugar snitched from Mom's kitchen, fed them fresh rootstock from bloodroot plants to sheen their appearance, gave them gentle commands as if he was asking the bank for a loan.

Neither my dad's care for his horse nor my chores were unusual. Most of my friends also were assigned chores that required us to "curry and brush, brush and curry" each horse at least once a day, feed each of them ear corn and oats every morning, corn, oats and hay at night, and make sure the dirt floors of their stalls were coated with straw a foot deep. Failure to notice a limp, a sore or any hint of illness could bring a reprimand from our fathers.

Most of us farm lads learned to bridle and harness the horses as eight-year-olds and to hitch them to farm equipment within a few months.

Horses were reliable and familiar. Tractors required new skills. Many farmers were reluctant to change and doubted whether mechanized horsepower was practical or economical. Their attitudes slowly changed.

Early tractors were lumbersome monsters that were difficult to steer, had no power lifts or power steering and required muscles to operate levers on cultivators and other attachments. An early model was the Fordson, short, squat and with a look that resembled pot-bellied Vietnamese pigs of a later era. Farmall, John Deere, Allis-Chalmers, Oliver, Minneapolis Moline, Case, Oliver, Avery and other makes of tractors followed.

The tractors allowed farmers to plow, disk, cultivate, run feed mills, silage cutters, buzz saws and other equipment. They changed agriculture, eliminated the need for some "hired hands" and allowed farmers to extend the acreage they would plant and harvest.

Our first tractor was a McCormick Deering F-20 with 4-inch deep lugs on steel wheels. It looked and seemed prehistoric compared to the Farmall H for which it was traded.

Dad had owned the F-20 for four or five years, but he was as excited as an eight-year-old with a store-bought kite that April morning in 1940 when the H arrived. He watched the truck driver back up to a creek bank, unchain the tractor and drive it onto the

Farmall H of the 1940s vintage
International Harvester Photo

bluegrass pasture. The tractor ran as smoothly as the Singer sewing machine Mom used.

Dad looked over the H while the trucker drove the old F-20 tractor onto the truck. The F-20 had served us well even though it had a crank instead of a starter, no battery or lights and could not be driven out on blacktop Ind. 58. It had been ideal for a field of new ground, where cut sapling stumps could have punctured a balloon tire.

The truck was barely through the gate before Dad was aboard the H. He stepped on the starter and the tractor sang out, each cylinder in tune. It was music to his ears. He drove the tractor to the tool shed and hitched the two-bottom plow that had arrived earlier.

A grin spread from ear to ear across his weather-wrinkled face as he drove to a field where I opened the gate. He drove 50 yards or so across the end of the field, turned to the right and pulled the trip, letting the plow slice into the clover sod. He shifted gears easily. The tractor hummed despite the weight of the two 12-inch plows as the points ripped through the loam, rolling the sod over the moldboard, exposing the cold underside to the warm sun.

Dad set his eyes on a fence post at the opposite end of the field so the furrow would be straight. He gripped the wheel, occasionally turning back to make sure the plows were going six to seven inches deep into the earth.

The upturned soil looked dark and rich and smelled as fresh as the April air. Our big collie followed in the furrow, curious about what was happening. Red worms wriggled from the ground to warm in the sun. For some, the heat was a death sentence. They vanished quickly into the beaks of birds that swooped down for a fresh meal.

Dad yanked the rope when he reached the end of the field and the plow raised slowly from the earth. He turned sharply before tripping the plow. Again it dug into the ground.

He pulled his dusty felt hat over his forehead, shielding his eyes from the sun that bounced off the bright red paint on the tractor's gas tank. Dad stayed aboard the tractor the rest of the afternoon, reluctant to stop even at 6 p.m. to do the milking.

He ate supper quickly, found a big cloth rag in the garage and walked back to the tool shed. He used the cloth to wipe the dirt off the tractor, trying to maintain the newness as long as possible.

Mom joined him after doing the dishes. She walked beside him to the field where he had plowed. "It's the best job of breaking ground I've ever done," he told her. They walked hand-in-hand back to the house, but not before taking one last look at the new H. It was spring, a time for renewal, a time for happiness.

Nothing could make a farmer happier than a new Farmall H, even if it meant demoting his beloved horses to a secondary role. The horses, however, remained important. They continued to pull the corn planter because, as Dad and other farmers agreed, tractors packed down the soil they had taken pains to work into silt."

Horses continued to be useful and their tender loving care did not end until the farmers reluctantly agreed to sell them and turn completely to mechanization.

Plowing Ahead

A year later, I still wasn't much bigger than a pound of lye soap, but being 12, I was sure I could handle that Farmall H. Dad wasn't nearly as certain, but I persisted until he suggested a compromise.

"If you can show me you're a man, I'll let you drive the tractor when we work the ground before planting corn," he said.

"How," I wondered, "can I do that?" I was not prepared for the answer he gave.

"You know that two- acre offset over on the west field," he asked, not waiting for an answer. "If you can take the team and plow that with a walking plow, it'll prove to me you're tough enough to operate the tractor."

It was the poorest, rockiest and most slopping patch on the farm. I am sure he expected me to decide to wait another year to drive the tractor rather than plow those two acres with the team.

Horse drawn walking plow
International Harvester Photo

But I was determined to drive that Farmall. The next morning I harnessed the horses and fastened the traces to the doubletree on the plow. I flipped the plow on its side, flicked the reins and drove the horses to the field.

Dad followed, feeling, I think, a bit guilty. He took the lines and drove the horses to open the first furrow. He showed me how to loop the reins around my neck and hold the plow.

"Be careful," he said. "This job is as tricky as licking honey off a thorn." He walked off, turned and yelled, "And be sure to let the horses rest now and then."

I was alone in an unfamiliar world with only the horses to talk to. I grasped the handles of the plow and lifted them slightly so the point would dig into the sod. I felt a sense of authority when the team responded to my commands. The plow point ripped a 12-inch wide strip loose from the earth and eased it up onto the moldboard. I noted the depth of the furrow, pleased it was at least the six to seven-inch depth Dad demanded.

"This is easy," I told myself. That was before the plow started hitting buried geodes and other rocks, springing each time from the furrow. And each time I backed the horses, reset the plow and continued, thankful the team was responsive to my commands.

Despite the interruptions, and the growing aches in my arms, the fresh smell of the mellow overturned earth gave a fitting welcome for a new growing season.

I declined Mom's suggestion to wait until the next morning to return to the field. Instead, I trudged on that afternoon and for a few hours the next day until the plot had been plowed.

Dad pointed out how the dead furrow could have been filled back in a little better than what I had done, but added. "Other than that I couldn't have done a better job myself." I am sure his comments were flattery.

He forgot the soreness in my arms and legs the next morning when he assigned me to disk one of the fields. "With the Farmall H."

I had grown up, or so I thought as I ran to the tractor. I was a long way from being a man, except in my Dad's eyes which was approval enough. It has been hard to match, ever, the emotion I felt that day atop that Farmall H.

A Time To Plant

Spring planting was a time for a farmer to dream of bountiful crops and for a boy to consider the meaning of seasons and the cycles of life.

Brother Wayne and I did a lot of dreaming on those May days in the late 1930s when we became old enough to go to the fields with Dad, a God-fearing man who believed he would reap what he sowed.

He disked and harrowed the fields until the soil sifted through his callused fingers like flour. Once the seed bed was ready, he parked the tractor and turned to the horses.

"Only way to plant is with a team," he explained, when we mentioned some neighbors were using tractors to pull their planters. The corn planter had been checked out days before to see that the plates at the bottom of the seed boxes would drop a grain of corn every 12 to 15 inches.

"Get corn any thicker than that, and we won't have nothin' but a bunch of nubbins if we get a dry spell this summer. This way, the stalks will be far enough apart to produce big ears a foot long," he added, that being a day before new hybrids made thicker stands possible. The fertilizer boxes were set to drop about 200 pounds an acre.

The horse-drawn corn planter sliced through the soft soil on two wheels, dropping the seed first, then the fertilizer, which were covered by the imprints of the wheels.

A marker that extended away from the planter on the unseeded part of the field indicated where the team would go on its next pass. We never ceased to be pleased at how straight the team and Dad planted the long rows.

The techniques of corn planting never changed. Our dreams did.

We could wile away 10 to 12 hours a day at one end of a field where the tractor and wagon were loaded with dozens of 80-pound bags of fertilizer, a few sacks of seed corn, a water keg for ourselves and two 10-gallon milk cans of water and some oats and corn for the horses.

Our job was to unstitch the burlap bags of 2-12-6 Rauh fertilizer, empty the contents into two big buckets and have them ready to pour into the containers atop the corn planter.

It was a continual chore that went on row after row, broken only for lunch when we replaced the bridles with halters and let the horses drink from big buckets before spreading their feed on the wagon bed. No one ate until the horses were served.

Once we settled into a routine of filling the fertilizer buckets, we could dream of what might or might never be.

Leaning back on a bag of seed corn, we watched the big foamy-looking clouds drift lazily overhead, wondered if they were the war clouds H. V. Kaltenborn kept talking about on the radio. We'd think about what war might be like, knowing only what we had read or heard some World War I veterans talk about.

We remembered mentions of mustard gas, the Maginot Line, barbed wire and deep trenches sometimes wet and soggy.

Sometimes we dreamed about the Empire State Building, which we knew was built of Indiana limestone, and wonder how high it reached.

When a rare plane eased across the horizon, we wondered about the emerging era of aviation. We'd look at the crows overhead scan the corn field and we wondered what it would be like to have wings. Those day dreams were endless, transitory thoughts that disappeared almost as quickly as they came to mind.

But never, ever, in our reverie did we consider the possibility of flights to the moon, travel in outer space or the vastness that awaited discovery beyond even our imaginations.

Contentment

Heaven to our neighbor Ben was 40 acres, a good wife, a team of horses and a cold drink. Ben never tried to get rich. All he wanted for himself was enough money to keep food on the table, a shirt on his back and a roof over the house.

He was cantankerous at times, kind and thoughtful on occasions. His little corner of the world was, as it had been for decades, on the slopes east of Heltonville. He farmed in the twilight of life almost the same as the first—with horse drawn implements and tender loving care for his crops.

Some neighbors told him, often it seemed, that time had passed him by, that he needed to modernize and mechanize to keep pace with the world that turned at an ever-quickening speed.

Ben paid them no heed. He was satisfied with his lot in life. He had what he sought, the contentment that others chased a lifetime and never caught. We saw that pleasure life gave him one June when we sat on a post holding up part of the fence that separated his farm from one of our fields.

Ben rode easily on the seat, holding freely the reins to the bridles on his team of horses as it pulled the two-row cultivator through the dark green corn. He wore a pair of bib overalls, patched on the knees with material that once had been a back pocket. One of the galluses was held in place with a No. 8 nail where a button was missing. He had a big red-patterned handkerchief around his neck and a dusty felt hat, once worn to church, on his head.

He looked down over the row of corn, making sure none of the plants had been covered by the cultivator. If they were he stopped the team, got off and carefully eased the dirt away and straightened the stalks.

We watched him do that several times and thought about the difference between how Dad and Ben worked. Dad was cultivating with the F-20 tractor that rumbled across the field at twice the speed of the horses. Although he was careful, there was no time, it appeared, for Dad to stop and uncover any corn.

We jumped off the post and walked over to Ben once when he stopped to give the horses a rest. We imprudently mentioned the difference in the way he farmed.

My impertinence did not bother Ben. He explained the reason clearly and thoughtfully.

"I'll tell you. Your pa has got kids at home. He tries to make sure he has money to buy each one of you the things you need and maybe some of the things you want but don't need.

"To do that, he has to farm as much land as he can. The more acres he farms, the more corn he grows and the more money he makes, unless it's a bad year and he loses more money.

"Now you take me and Ellie," Ellie being his wife. "We don't have kids and no one depends on us for help. You see what I mean?" he asked, wiping his forehead with the handkerchief.

He went on, "Your dad has a lot more responsibility than I have. He has a family to feed. All I've got to do is raise enough corn to pay my property taxes, feed a couple of pigs, milk that old Jersey out there and gather eggs from the Rhode Island Reds in the chickenhouse.

"And raise a good garden. That gives Ellie and me all we need. The farm's paid for and all I owe is my parents for putting me here on the green earth and the Good Lord for takin' care of us."

We nodded, "Talk to you later," he said, flipping the reins just lightly enough to tell the horses it was time to return to work.

Taste of Threshing

Only a few combines that both cut and threshed grain (soybeans had not yet become a major crop) were in use in our area in the 1930s. Farmers still cut the crops with binders, which kicked out twine-knotted bundles that were shocked in fields. The crop would then await the arrival of a hulking threshing machine towed, usually, by a lumbering steam engine.

Neighbors swapped help as the thresher went from farm to farm where it was anchored in place and linked to the steam engine or giant tractor with a wide belt that ran between pulleys on each machine.

Shocks of wheat were hauled on flatbed wagons from the fields to the thresher where it was fed onto a conveyor. Inside the thresher a series of screens and shakers divided straw from grain. Grain was emptied into wagons or bagged, the straw blown into huge stacks that glistened in the sun.

Serendipity, we were told, would come later when we looked for a needle in a strawstack and found the farmer's daughters. If anyone experienced serendipity he was wise enough not to mention it.

It was fortunate, at the time of threshing rings, that diet had not yet become a four-letter buzz word. The wheat harvest meant bounteous food and tables fit for a king. Big meals, loaded with starch, soaked in fat, rich in sugar and high in carbohydrates were in vogue. It was more stylish it seemed to have a physique that looked more like a barrel than a rail.

Cholesterol was of no concern. Doctors didn't show their patients their lipid profiles to make them think they were on the road to Undertakerville. Most of the men—and women too—expended enough physical energy to offset fats, red meats and sweets.

Triglycerides, for all we knew, could have been a name for a hillbilly band playing over at the Shady Springs roadhouse on U.S. 50.

Food was cheap—and plentiful—on farms around Heltonville where folks were forced into self-sufficiency by the economics of the times.

Labor, too, was plentiful, but there was little, if any, money to pay for it. Into this void came the threshing crew, an organized, efficient hard-working group of men who traded one good day's work for another.

And their wives made the circuit, too, going from farm to farm, helping prepare noontime meals for the 30-40 men. And for boys, who found it the best season of their lives.

We went wherever our parents went. We rotated the jobs. One day we might bag the grain, the next tie the sack, the third carry fresh, cool water from springs in wooden kegs and heavy jugs. We felt we were involved in something bigger than ourselves.

We tried to be at the farm houses in time to see the men arrive for dinner, which was the rural term for lunch. We liked to see the farmers, big men in bib overalls and denim shirts, pull handkerchiefs a yard square from their hip pockets and whip the dirt and sweat from their faces, walk to a row of big granite washpans, pour in water from galvanized 10-quart buckets, cup their soap-coated hands, douse their craggy faces and rub briskly.

It mattered not that they did a poor job of scrubbing. There were plenty of towels made from feed sacks to wipe away the rest of the dirt.

Inside the houses or under the shade of trees, long tables were fashioned on saw horses, barrels and assorted blocks. The tables were loaded with enough food for an entire township, on the menu big chunks of beef, pork and ham, piles of fried chicken, sausage cakes, foot-long roasting ears, fresh green beans, peas, beets, deviled eggs, slaw, apple butter, homemade butter, an assortment of breads and always big bowls of mashed potatoes and thick whole milk gravy.

The host farmer waited until each man and boy was seated, then chose someone to say grace, which at times was no more than "Good bread, good meat, good God, let's eat. Amen." It may have seemed irreverent, but it was not meant to be and the Lord probably didn't let it bother Him anymore than the farmers did.

The wives waited, ready to fill any dish that might be nearly empty. The men ate with gusto, pleased that the threshing ring allowed them feasts day after day for two weeks, sometimes three, but never on Sundays.

Once they finished what they called the "meat and taters" course, the wives brought out the desserts, chocolate and angel food cakes; apple, gooseberry, rhubarb, peach pies; cobblers of various fruits and vanilla and banana pudding.

Once finished, the workers sprawled on the grass, dotted with plantain and buckhorn, to "let our food settle." It seemed to settle quickly for they soon were back at work.

As they departed, the women gathered the leftovers. It was not uncommon to hear them comment, "Well, I swan. They ate every bite of my meatloaf." Another woman would add, "Glory be. Ain't no greater compliment a woman can get than to have a man like her cookin'."

That being the case, not a woman went home without being complimented. It was praise they heard day after day until all the wheat had been threshed.

The Combine Appears

Dad didn't realize how much the threshing ring was part of his life until after he agreed to have Thornt Clampitt combine his wheat crop near the end of the 1930s.

Thornt's new tractor-drawn John Deere, a novelty at the time, cut a six-foot swath through wheat, oats and rye, separating the grain from the straw in one trip through the field.

Dad conceded the "big green machine" was likely the wave of the future. It eliminated the need to cut the crop with a binder, shock the bundles, then wait for the threshing machine to make its rounds.

He was impressed when neighbors gathered almost as soon as Thornt arrived with the combine, which reaped a 17-acre field of wheat in what seemed like no time at all. Other onlookers were amazed at the speed.

Dad decided later the harvest should have taken a little longer. His doubting neighbors kneeled on their knees and pulled away the straw to expose grains of wheat that had dropped onto the ground instead of going into the hopper on the combine.

"Looks like the reel done beat out the grain before it got on the canvas," one of them said.

Dad defended the operation the best he could. "Can't expect perfection the first year," he told them, adding: "You all will be sorry when you're out threshing and I'm sittin' in the shade whittlin'.

Dad lost his interest in "whittlin' as soon as he saw the threshing machine rumble down the gravel road. He waited until his neighbors were out of sight to check out the grain that remained on the ground. Any profit he had expected from the crop had been left on the floor of the field.

Already distressed, he soon realized he would not be a part of the summer ritual. Missing the threshing ring would be like a July without a Fourth to celebrate.

Even though his crop was harvested, the steam engine called and he answered, showing up with the horses and wagon to help when it reached a nearby farm. Other farmers looked surprised. "Didn't expect to see you," one of the men said, taunting, "We thought you might spend the day whittlin'."

Dad ignored the derision. "Figured if there was work to be done, I ought to help with it," he replied.

And help he did. He worked as hard as anyone, stacking bundles of wheat as they were thrown onto his wagon, then taking them to the threshing machine.

A few men razzed him some more at noon about helping when he didn't have to. Dad just forked another piece of fried chicken and an ear of corn and said, "Wouldn't be summer without this food the women folk fix for us threshers."

The threshing ring continued for another year or two. By then World War II was under way, time was more important than tradition and combines were improved to prevent much of the grain from being left on the ground.

And a part of an annual farm tradition ended. And in time, Dad bought his own combine and made sure it put the wheat in the hopper, not on the ground.

Hay Harvest

Except for early alfalfa cuttings, hay making usually followed the wheat harvest. Much of the work was done by hand, the hay mowed and raked with machines, then lofted onto wagons to a stacker by men with pitckforks.

Oh a few mechanical loaders pulled behind a wagon were around but most farmers rated them as "more trouble than worth."

A few stationery balers were in use but those pulled by tractors and picked up the hay from windrows were rare until after the war ended. Loading wagons was routine, the real excitement came at the barn.

Wagons were pulled, one at a time, to the front of the barn where a hay fork dangled from a thick rope that ran up to the apex of the roof where a track extended along the peak of the rafters the length of the barn.

The fork were varied. Some were straight with two points that were stuck in the hay; ours was a four-point cradle that spread four feet when opened. My dad took pride in being able to unload a big wagon with only four forkfuls.

Meantime, another worker had driven a team of horses to the other end of the barn, hitched it to the doubletrees to which the one-inch thick hay rope was attached. He waited until Dad "stuck" the fork and three hired hands were in the hayloft.

Once all were in place, Dad yelled "Okay," loud enough for it to be heard on the other end of the barn, a signal that the rope could be pulled by the horses. Slowly the hayfork with its load rose to the top of the barn, entered the track and rumbled across the barn on its steel road.

Once the hay had reached the desired location in the barn, one of the men inside would bellow, "dump it." It was signal for the horses to be stopped and for Dad to pull a rope tripping the fork, sending the hay onto the loft to be thrown into place by the workers there.

Those steps were followed until each wagon was unloaded and new loads brought to the barn.

As the day wore on the dust and the heat of summer grew worse. Shirts became wet with sweat, the stone jug with the corncob stopper ran out of water quickly and was refilled frequently.

It was hard work and it could be dangerous inside the barn as the hay rose higher and higher. Wasps from nests against the roof sought to protect their domain and did not hesitate to bury their stingers into the workers.

An afternoon break was a welcome relief. As the men gathered outside the spring house, Dad carried out a watermelon cooled in the water. It popped open in front of his big pocket knife, which was used to slice each worker the slabs they savored, disregarding the juice that ran from the corners of their mouths. Once the respite ended, they returned to the hay field, even though the sun was its hottest.

Once the chores were done Mom handed us towels made from chicken feed sacks and ordered us to go to the creek to wash. We expect the same order was given the other workers. Dust was for field and barn, not for the house.

Ornery Chores

Other summer farm chores were even more onerous, among them picking wild berries, mowing fence rows and cleaning chicken houses.

Berries meant chiggers and scratches and hours of work with little to show for it. They were small, so small it seemed to take an hour to fill the bottom of a 10-quart bucket, an afternoon to fill one.

Walking home from picking berries in a thicket one afternoon, a farmer offered me a ride on the drawbar of his tractor. The ride was welcome . . . until the tractor hit a bump, freeing the bail of my bucket from my sweaty hand, dumping the fruits of my labor onto a county road which by that time of year was more dust than gravel. I had nothing to show for my efforts. I am not sure my mom ever believed my story, likely thinking I had spent the time staying cool in a pool in the creek.

Most men took pride in their farms and kept fence rows mowed out to the roads. Rocks and gravel could damage mowing machine blades, which in turn could harm fences, meaning scythes—the kind operated by arm power—were used.

It was hard work, but tolerable for anyone who was immune to poison ivy, yellow jackets, bumble bees and snakes that sometimes hissed when their territories were invaded.

Among the worst jobs was cleaning chicken houses, which usually was done in the fall when older laying hens were sold to make room for pullets that were beginning to lay. Most hen houses had low roofs, floors coated with straw and roosts (often round sassafras poles two-inches in diameter) that were over the nests.

Stinking droppings had to be scooped from under the roosts, carried to a door and tossed into a manure spreader. The heat of the roof and the scent of the load mounted with each trip. Both could be tolerated. Cleaning the worn straw from the floor was worse. Dust, streaked with rivulets of sweat, coated our faces, often sending us gasping outside for relief.

We grew even filthier once that was done when we used brushes and buckets of used motor oil to coat the roosts. The oil, we were told, would keep the lice from the hen house. It would not, unfortunately, keep out the dust or prevent the roost to be littered.

Our parents told us that what did not kill us would make us stronger. We never learned what strength we gained from that ordeal.

In the years that followed chicken houses all but disappeared from farms, so did fences as farms grew larger. A few people, however, still pick berries, but that must be their own form of self-punishment.

Butchering

Unless we were sick our parents did not let us skip school except for an emergency, one of which came on a December day in the early 1940s.

A neighbor who always helped us butcher hogs begged off the night before my parents planned to butcher two 200-pound hogs. "Feeling puny," he explained, puny being a rural term for "under the weather."

"Think you're man enough to help?" I was asked. "You kiddin?" I asked. "I can hold up my end."

Dad laughed. "We will see how your end is holdin' up by the end of tomorrow." By, then, considering his inexperienced help for the day, he had decided to butcher but one hog.

"Tomorrow" started at 4:30 a.m. when I was told to fill two huge black kettles with water, then build a fire under them with kindling and wood. Dad fed the animals and milked the cows in the meantime.

The sun rose bright and clear, the temperature, in the teens, ideal for their job ahead.

A single shot brought down the Chester White barrow. I winced at the sound and pulled my jacket around my neck, but I was wise enough to know the lives of farm animals were short and purposeful.

From then on, we went through the steps of butchering almost automatically. Boys from cities might not have endured some of the tasks that had to be done, but I was familiar with the routine.

By noon the most difficult work was behind us. The rest would be routine and much of it could be done indoors.

Mom helped trim the hams and made sure they were ready to be hung in the smokehouse to cure. Each of us sliced the fat into small cubes, which were heated in a kettle and then squeezed in a press that forced out the liquid that would set into lard when emptied into large tin cans.

I knew the cracklin's that were left would be good when warm, but not nearly as savory as the long strip of tenderloin that was among the stacks of meat. Sausage was good, bacon okay, tenderloin mouth-watering.

We dined on slices of tenderloin, pinto beans, mashed potatoes and pumpkin pie at supper, but the meat for sausage still had
to be cranked through the grinder that was attached to a long
board from where the meat dropped into a huge pan.

I turned the grinder while Mom dropped meat into it. She
wanted all-meat sausage and any pieces with excessive fat were
laid aside for another use.

Fresh sausage and gravy sent me on the way to school the
next morning.

I expected some harsh words from the principal, but he
smiled when he said, "Your excuse would be a lot easier to accept
if you'd brought some of that sausage in with you."

Lye Soap

Men who had any smarts at all didn't get involved in
soapmaking. That was a job the women preferred to do themselves. It wasn't that it was easy work. It wasn't. It took talent,
the kind men were too impatient to learn.

Soap making was a task that came after hogs were butchered
because the grease from fat was a major ingredient needed for the
end product.

Like butchering, it was a chore that required a kettle, the kind
that rested on a metal ring connected to three metal legs. Most husbands built the needed fire then stepped inside to let the women
take charge. Cold fat chunks sizzled as they were tossed into the
warm kettle. Water was added from time to time and the contents
stirred slowly with a wooden paddle well-worn from previous use.

The stirring kept the lard scraps from scorching if stuck to
the bottom of the kettle. Certain the fat had been cooked into
grease, the wife took a long-handled pan and dipped out the
cracklings, which were what was left of the scraps. Only the
grease remained.

To make lye soap, lye was needed, an amount equal to the fat,
which could be two, maybe three, cans. The stirring with the paddle resumed, slowly, constantly, to make certain the lye and the
grease were mixing. By instinct, or by experience, a soapmaker
knew when a batch of soap was done.

That's when she looked around for a chicken feather, which she pulled through a cloth to clean, then gingerly dipped it into the lye and grease. It remained briefly, then was removed. If only the quill was left, the mixture was strong and the contents had cooked long enough.

Contents were dipped from the kettle into heavy cardboard boxes, that allowed for three-inch thick bars to hardened into soap, golden in color, heavy in weight, smelly in scent and coarse in texture.

It wasn't the kind of soap to put in a wrapper and leave on the tub at the Greystone Hotel in Bedford. And it didn't do much for complexions, but no teenager who used it ever had a problem with acne.

Lye soap made thick, heavy suds for the laundry and was good in dish water. It was better than "a lot of the weak stuff store sold," wives said. "And a lot cheaper," said their conservative spending husbands.

And sassy kids soon learned it was not wise to be impudent with parents who used lye soap to wash out the mouths of mouthy brats.

Buzz Words

If the Occupational Safety and Health Administration had been around in the 1930s and 1940s, half the population of Lawrence County might have frozen to death.

OSHA never would have allowed youngsters to work around buzz saws the way they did without an assortment of safety devices. And the buzz saws were what cut the wood that provided the fuel for stoves that heated the farm homes.

Chain saws had not yet made their appearance. And without buzz saws, the task of cutting enough wood to warm the big, rambling, uninsulated houses would have been long and laborious.

Buzz saws were round, 30-36 inches in diameter, and were driven by a belt from a pulley on the tractor to a pulley on the saw rig. Others were mounted on a platform that had to be anchored in the ground. Others were attached to the front of tractors.

Our rig, as I recall, was designed by Jim East at his blacksmith shop in Heltonvllle to fit on the front of the Farmall H. Two pieces of steel were bolted to the tractor's frame, each piece extending out about six feet. An axle fitted across the two pieces of steel. It held the pulley on one side, a place for the buzz saw on the opposite side.

Buzz saws had teeth that cut across the wood with a zinging sound that echoed off barn roofs and bounced off hills across the hollows. To Dad, the reverberations were music to his ear, the pitch and vibration changing with the hardness of the wood. Oak, beech and other hardwoods made the zing louder and sharper, sassafras, poplar and softwood lessened the vibrations.

The rig on the tractor meant wood could be cut from tree tops in the woods where timber had been "harvested" or in the wood lot where we had hauled long pieces of wood on the wagon.

One person could saw wood on the rig, but three workers tripled the output in the same amount of time.

Brother Wayne held the poles as Dad sawed off fire wood 16 to 18 inches long. My job usually was to "offbear," which meant I held the short piece of wood being cut, then flipped it into the pile or into a wagon. I had to stand within two to three feet of the saw and hold my hands within inches as it rotated at hundreds of revolutions per minute.

I never did feel too comfortable at the task, but Dad told me, "That's good. If you start feeling like you're equal to the saw, you're way too overconfident." We could cut cord after cord, working harmoniously, stopping only when one of us got sawdust in his eyes or needed a drink of water from a nearby creek.

Once in awhile, Dad would let us feed the saw to get the knack of it. None of us ever got hurt, or came close to it. But that was because we knew the saw was boss and master and not to trifled with. The work did give us a sense of confidence, a feeling of pride knowing we could stare danger in the eye and never blink.

We always laughed when we left for school the following Monday and Mom would remind us at least twice, "Be careful boys. And watch your step."

HOME LIFE

Lamp Lights

Most farms in our area in the 1930s had no electricity, central heat, air conditioning, refrigeration, plumbing, water, hot or cold, from a tap.

It didn't bother us at the time, but the absence of electricity seemed ridiculous in hindsight. Public Service Indiana transmission lines ran across our farm as it did those of neighbors, yet the PSC did not serve us, probably after learning the returns would be less than the cost. "Public service," then as now does not always mean public service.

Home of the author through high school

That public service was left to the Rural Electrification Administration and its rural electric cooperatives. The Jackson County REMC was given the right to extend across the line into our area of Lawrence County, but World War II delayed the work. It took dozens of pleas for the service... and even explanations for why it couldn't be done... once the war ended. It was 1948 before the REMC turned on the lights in our part of the country.

Heat in winter came to lower level rooms from the kitchen range and a wood stove. Flat irons and heated bricks wrapped in towels kept our feet warm until we fell asleep in upstairs bedrooms. Water sometimes froze in the water glasses beside our beds.

Upstairs rooms under tin roofs could be as hot in summer as they were cold in winter. An air conditioner was a hand fan with an advertisement for the Jones Funeral Home in Heltonville. In the torrid summer of the mid-1930s, some people claimed they sought relief in the cool dankness of area caves. We sometimes chose the front porch, ignoring any nocturnal pests that might feed on our bodies.

Water came from the spring, its cool water basin refrigeration for milk, butter and cream. A cistern that captured rainfall provided water for the laundry. Personal relief was a hundred or so steps out a path well beyond the house.

If there were hardships it didn't seem so at the time. Life is best lived when adjusted to its circumstances.

Parental Power

Farm boys who grew up in the 1930s had, as mentioned, a special bond with their fathers. They turned to their mothers when things didn't go right.

Fathers taught them how to mend fence, plow, plant, harvest, cut wood, and care for the land and the things that lived on it.

Mothers showed them how to pick berries, make a garden, separate cream from milk, dress neatly, be humble, and care about people as well as things.

Boys sought approval from their fathers, love from their mothers.

Fathers were their friends, advisers, confidants. Mothers were their disciplinarians, making them walk the line when their fathers were too permissive.

Fathers taught sons the work ethic, the belief that success belonged to those who earned it. Mothers taught them that work was important and success admirable, but that there also was more to life.

Fathers gave them farm machinery instructions to read. Mothers handed them good magazines and great books.

Fathers bought them bib overalls, high top boots and pocket knives. Mothers saw to it they had dress pants, clean shoes for church and pocket combs.

Fathers made sure they were up at dawn to help with the chores. Mothers made certain they were ready when the school bus came.

Fathers looked upset when their report cards were bad. Mothers appeared disappointed.

Fathers said, "boys will be boys" when they got into trouble. Mothers cried.

Fathers accepted the fact their sons sometimes wanted to skip church on Sunday mornings. Mothers fretted about their salvation.

Fathers would rant and rage when they did a job poorly or carelessly. Mothers reminded them gently, "Anything worth doing is worth doing well."

Fathers had the answers to their questions. Mothers posed questions and let them search for the answers.

Fathers were sometimes caustic, sometimes scathing. Mothers were, it seemed, always even-tempered and gentle.

Fathers rebuked them at times, making them angry enough to want to leave home. Mothers told them, "Dads have bad days like everyone else. By tomorrow everything will be all right." And it usually was for Mothers were more often right than wrong.

Fathers wanted sons to make things easier for their mothers. Mothers wanted the boys to help ease their fathers' burdens.

Boys bragged to other boys about their fathers. Mothers were taken for granted. But they never complained.

Memo To Moms

This is a Mother's Day message I wrote years back, not to mothers, but to their sons. It was intended for any son who grew up in a rural area in the 1930s:

Our mothers are gone and there are no phones or mail service where they now dwell. It is too bad. Maybe now that we have lived two-thirds of a lifetime ourselves we can express what they meant to us.

They departed ten, twenty, thirty years ago, but they remain a part of us, indelible memories that cannot be erased from the recesses of our minds.

A button pops off a shirt and we think back to the time they would slowly thread a needle and sew it back.

They darned our socks, mended the rips in our clothes, then washed them over a scrubboard in a tub of hot water when the gasoline engine on the Maytag washer wouldn't start.

The washing always was done on Monday. They never missed, rain or shine. It was as certain as church on Sundays. They used homemade lye soap and bluing to remove the dirt and grease we accumulated messing around machinery, doing chores and working in the fields.

On Tuesdays, they pressed our overalls and work shirts with irons heated on the kitchen range. They knew the clothes would soon be wrinkled and dirty, but they still made them look good.

They baked, worked in the garden, picked berries, cut the rhubarb, worked on quilts, churned and did whatever needed to be done the rest of the week. Each day, they would be the first to rise, the bacon they sizzled sending out a wake-up call to the rest of the household.

They helped with the milking, worried over the baby chicks like mother hens, and wondered whether the eggs they gathered would bring what money they expected when the huckster wagon arrived. They had dinner waiting at noon when we stopped what we were doing. Somehow they found time to read the morning paper and then relate the news to us while we stuffed ourselves.

They always sliced the smallest piece of pie for themselves and, even then, they'd offer it to us if we wanted a second or third.

It was the same at supper. They washed the dishes in a dishpan with water heated in a teakettle and dried them with a towel that had once been part of a sack that held the chicken feed.

When we became upset with our dads, or they with us, it was our moms who were the mediators. They listened to us, then our fathers, somehow managing to make us each feel better without taking sides.

They stewed while our sisters were out on dates and stayed up until we got home, even until we were 15 or 16.

They were hurt when we sometimes begged off going to prayer meetings or revivals and wondered about our salvation. We did other things they didn't approve of, but always they forgave us. Maybe that was because we cared enough about them not to embarrass them often.

They shaped our lives and our values. We were too wrapped up with ourselves, though, to let them really know how much they meant to us.

But somehow we think they knew. Moms had perceptions that let them understand more about us than we wanted them to know.

Kick Start Laundry

For farm wives a Maytag was a Cadillac of washing machines. They thought they'd died and gone to heaven when a delivery driver arrived with one in the 1930s.

Husbands saved a dollar here, a dime there to buy the machines as presents for special occasions. It didn't matter if the washers had gasoline engines and had to be started with a foot pedal since the Rural Electrification Administration had yet to turn on the lights in the country.

Most wives had assumed they would continue to scrub clothes by hand on a washboard in a tub at least until the depression ended. The women wasted no time putting the washers to work. Most had hot water aboil in big black kettles by dawn and clothes awash before the children left for school. By noon the clothes were hanging bright and clean from the lines that stretched across yards.

Over the years, the Maytags worked well, easily started easily maintained. Like all things mechanical, though, they eventually became difficult to start. Wives tried and failed, so did their husbands. Mechanics tinkered with the engines and fixed them for a while before they again refused to run.

Electricity, as noted, reached most farms in the late 1940s. So did indoor plumbing and running water. And so did delivery drivers with new electric Maytags.

Farm wives thought they had died and gone to heaven for a second time. And their husbands were elated they no longer would be tormented by a gasoline engine that wouldn't start.

Huckster Truck

He drove a creaking, rocking huckster truck that brought the city to the country.

He was George to his customers, Mr. Hunsucker to their children.

George's truck rumbled through the countryside Monday through Saturday, taking a different route from Louden's store in Bedford each day.

George stopped at 45 to 50 homes on each route, making friends for himself, profits for the Louden boys, Harmon and Pryce. Everything George sold came with a smile and an affordable price.

Folks in the Mundell community east of Heltonville awaited George's visit each Thursday. They could spot his truck in the dry summer months by the dust storm it whipped up as it rumbled over roads built of clay and creek gravel. When March arrived, they could hear the truck laboring through ruts in the roads that had become quagmires after the thaw.

The Chevy didn't always make it through the mud. When it didn't, George would ram the gearshift into reverse, back up, stick the transmission into low and floor-board it through the muck. Once or twice a week, that didn't work. He remained mired down until a farmer used a team of horses or mules to yank the truck to a firm footing.

Wes and Edith waited for George to show up, no matter how long it took. They bought big jars of peanut butter, eight loaves of bread, sacks of sugar and assorted groceries from George. When he'd found all the foodstuffs they needed, he stepped down from the truck, grabbed a can Wes held and filled it with kerosene. The kerosene was for the lamps in the house and lanterns in the barn.

"Don't forget my mash," Edith would remind George. George returned with a big bag from the back corner of the truck and set it on the ground. The mash was for the chickens, the sack it came in material for a dress or towels.

George would then tote up the bill, take an order for the following week, and ask, "Anything you want to trade today?"

Trade might be eggs or cream. A couple of times a year, Edith sold chickens, fryers once the males were separated from the pullets, old hens later when the pullets began to lay. That meant George would have to return at night in another truck loaded with coops and ask for help in catching the chickens in the hen house.

It was much the same at the other small farms except at Jimmy Martin's house, where Mrs. Martin usually had lunch ready. Most times she and Jimmy demanded that they be joined by George and his wife, Helen, who at times accompanied him.

George passed on news from one house to the other, but he never betrayed trusts. He told us later he was once stopped by a youngster who said he wanted to buy a pack of cigarettes for an older friend.

"What's his name?" George asked.

"Don't know," the boy confessed, sheepishly.

George sold him the cigarettes.

"Don't tell my folks," the boy pleaded.

"Just don't tell you bought them from me," George replied.

A few years later, huckster wagons passed from the scene. Rural families could drive into town to shop for the things George had delivered. They found everything they wanted, except friendship like his. The Hunsuckers later moved to Indianapolis where George worked as an electrician until he retired.

CHURCHES/RELIGION

All-Day Meetings

Rural churches were more than houses of worship. They were social centers, places to meet old friends and make new ones, places to be married, celebrate births and mourn the dead.

They provided playgrounds for new generations, graveyards for generations past. They were sanctuaries for those needing aid and comfort and for those in search of the meanings of life and death.

The busiest day of the year came in mid-summer. Some churches called day-long observances, "homecomings," others referred to them as reunions or basket dinners.

At Mundell, southeast of Heltonville, the second Sunday in July was an all-day meeting. It was a day each of us 11-year-olds awaited in 1940, not because of the morning and afternoon services, but because of the basket dinner at noon.

We fidgeted through the opening of services, waiting for superintendent Nolan Bowman to announce we could go to our Sunday School classes. We behaved in Miss Cummings' class, knowing she might tell our mothers if we acted badly.

That, however, was all the regimentation we could take. We didn't return to the sanctuary for the sermon when Sunday School classes ended, fleeing instead to the outdoors to romp under the shade trees. We kept our voices low, lest an adult leave the church to muffle our shouts.

An hour later the men came from the church, leaving wives inside to set the tables in the basement.

No one—man or boy—had to be called twice when the food was ready. We shuffled our feet during what seemed like a lengthy prayer, aware that young people would be allowed to go through the line first.

We never kept the adults behind us waiting long. We piled our plates with fried chicken, ham, beef, fresh corn-on-the-cob, apple butter, homemade biscuits and everything else except vegetables.

We used our free hands to hold tall glasses of lemonade, then stepped outside to find a cool place to eat. We always went back for seconds. The third time was for desserts—a big slice of apple pie, a scoop or two of banana pudding, a piece of chocolate cake.

"Threshing machines," adults called our ability to devour bite after bite. No matter. Our appetites were never a match for the amount of food available for the taking.

We skipped the afternoon sermon, preferring to read the engravings on tombstones or meander through Charlie Mark's poplar grove across the road.

It was after 4 p.m. before we left the church. Evening chores were ahead but we had time to check the leftovers in mom's dinner basket. The basket, we were happy to note, held enough desserts to last until an ice cream social later in the week.

A Greater Power

A friend's experience has never been forgotten. He was at the age of skepticism and doubt about what he had learned in Sunday school. He relayed his questions about the value of church and the teachings he heard there.

His dad looked hurt, but he didn't make a big speech or quote Scripture or repeat any of the sermons the preacher delivered.

He just said quietly, "Let's go for a walk, Son." They strolled together, climbed over a slat gate into the corn field where the corn was ankle-high. It had been a good spring and the wind whipped the leaves on the small stalks into a sea of dark green.

His dad said, "Take a long look at this field and tell me this is all the work of me and you alone. Or the accumulation of all the help others have given us." He looked skyward, then said: "We don't make the rain or the sun or perform the magic that can turn one grain of corn into a stalk that produces one or two ears, each with 400-500 grains."

They crossed another fence into a field of red clover, lush and awaiting the mower. A small bag of seeds, none bigger than a speck, would yield a hundred bales or more of hay.

They walked to the orchard where the earliest apples were taking shape.

The father talked about the seasons, how each spring brought new life that yielded its produce in the summer, relaxed in the fall, went dormant in winter and was reborn in spring in a never-ending cycle.

They watched a young mother bird bring worms to her nest of young, a newborn calf find sustenance, instinctively, from its mother.

The father talked about the land and the things on it, the son seldom interrupting to ask questions. He was learning by listening.

As they returned to the house, his dad asked, "Well, do you still doubt there is Someone greater than me, or you, or any other human being will ever encounter on earth?"

The boy could have added that to his doubts, but he smiled knowingly in return. It had been a walk well spent for the boy . . . and for the father.

No Place To Hide

As teens, we learned—embarrassingly—not even to appear to criticize the religion others seek to follow.

Three of us, debating how to spend a Sunday evening, agreed to sit in on a service at a fundamentalist church north of Heltonville. "Holy-Rollers," members the congregation were called by some people who attended more traditional churches.

Our curiosity was taken as disapproval.

The church was not a grand edifice. It was a modest frame building with a tin roof. It rested on a foundation two or three feet above the ground atop block corner stones.

The service was uneventful for a while until a woman in her early 20s arose to "testify." She related her background, then told in vivid detail about her experience with men. She was explicit, leaving little to our imagination. Innocent beyond our year, our faces turned a blistering crimson and we were thankful we were in the back pew and ignored by those to the front.

Within minutes she was talking in tongues, her language stranger than her behavior before she collapsed onto the floor. It appeared to be a familiar scene to others. It was new to us.

We thought we had escaped notice. Another youth we had not seen in his front row seat rose to offer his testimony. He made a few remarks, then to our dismay, pointed toward us and said, "Lord, those three boys in the back row are here to make fun of us. They don't understand our faith. They are here to smirk at what we do and what we say."

We slipped down in our seats, hoping and praying, the floor would drop from the church and free us from a hundred pairs of eyes. Too stunned to move we stayed put, even when the collection plate was passed.

The pile of bills, $5s, $10, even a few $20s, rose from the plate. We had seen collections at our own churches, in less depressed areas, but they had never appeared as large. These were true believers who gave to their Lord more than they could afford to give to themselves. We were impressed with their faith.

Once the benediction had been said, we bolted for the door and sped to the car, agreeing almost in unison to never do that again.

We were wiser because of the experience and forever tolerant of those who choose to worship in whatever ways they choose.

Foot In Mouth

Zeke could criticize his kids, but nobody else better do so. Rev. Jones found that out. Those names are aliases, their real ones best unmentioned, because their identities are unimportant to the story.

Zeke was a farmer near Heltonville, as much a pillar to the community and the church he attended as anyone else.

Rev. Jones was a part-time preacher on Sundays, a high school principal on weekdays at another county school that was one of Heltonville's biggest rivals. He had three reasons for preachin' and teachin'. The church needed a pastor, the Lord told him to work Sundays and, like most folks, he needed the extra money.

Zeke and Rev. Jones never had much rapport, but they tolerated each other for the good of the church. They did, that is, until the minister said something he should have left unsaid one Sunday after church.

He and Zeke were talking when Zeke's younger son walked up. The boy played basketball at Heltonville and, although Zeke seldom saw a game, he didn't figure either of his boys could do anything wrong.

Heltonville had played the high school where the Rev. Jones was principal the previous Friday night, winning by a narrow margin.

The pastor put his arm on the boy's shoulder and said, "That was a good ball game the other night." The boy expressed his thanks.

That's when Rev. Jones put his foot in his mouth, adding: "That No. 11 on your team was sure a dirty player, though."

Zeke frowned, looked at Ned and asked, "Ain't No. 11 your brother, son?"

"Yep, that's the number he wears," the younger son replied.

Zeke didn't often lose his temper, certainly not on the church grounds. But he did then. He looked at Rev. Jones and said, harshly: "My boys don't play dirty, preacher man. If you say they do you're wrong and you ain't got no business bein' a minister."

He added a few more words, the likes of which the church yard had never heard, before he was grabbed by the arm and pulled away, yelling over his shoulder to the bewildered Rev. Jones:

"As long as you're the preacher here I won't be back."

Zeke was true to his word. He missed church the next Sunday for the first time in years. And the Sunday after that and the Sunday after that. He continued to drive his wife to church, then return to pick her up. But he continued to bristle, complaining because the Rev. Jones was preachin' the Gospel according to the Rev. Jones.

Some of Zeke's friends thought he must be right if he was so adamant. They stopped going to church, too, and soon contributions barely covered the bottom of the collection baskets. Through "an agreement mutually satisfactory to both the minister and the church board," the Rev. Jones submitted his resignation.

The church hired another preacher and Zeke resumed his attendance. And as far as was known the preacher never again complained about the son of a parishioner being an unfair player.

Gravediggers

A cemetery was as much for the living as for the dead. At least, it seemed that way at Mundell Cemetery as Decoration Day neared. It became even more obvious if a grave had to be dug.

The graveyard was next to the church in a farm community a few miles southeast of Heltonville. It was a place where neighbors looked after one another, a place where visitors went from strangers to friends in the time it took to say "howdy." No one ever had to hire a grave dug in the 1930s and early 1940s. The work was done by the farmers, who thought nothing of taking time off from field work to show up at the cemetery, mattocks and shovels in hand.

They worked for nothing, but they were paid for their effort in something worth more than money. The pay came in the form of an inner richness that made them feel good about themselves and the other men around them.

It was a ritual to honor a departed friend or a tribute to a former neighbor who had moved away, but had asked to be buried in the cemetery.

We tagged along to the graveyard whenever we could, as did other third and fourth graders. It was a place even at our ages we knew we could learn about life as well as death.

We soon learned who were the workers and who were the talkers at the grave site. Some of the men said little while they waited to jump down into the grave, drive a mattock in the earth time after time, then throw the dirt onto a mound above. Others talked a lot while they waited, then complained about how hard the ground was once they started to shovel.

Men who barely knew the person who was to be buried talked a lot about him, exalting him, making him seem more of a friend than he actually had been. Others who knew the deceased much better, said little. Their loss was written in the wrinkles on their weathered faces.

We enjoyed listening when the men relived the lives of a departed neighbor. They told stories about him, good-natured memories that caused them to reflect on the man and his accomplishments.

The grave-digging took a half-day, sometimes longer, giving those of us too young to work time to walk through the cemetery, reading gravestones bleached by the sun and worn by the rain. The tombstones were lessons in history, a march of time, a record of the men and women who had come and gone, leaving their marks on the places they lived.

Some pre-Decoration Day visitors stopped to talk to the men at work. Some went quickly to a gravestone, left a bouquet of flowers, looked solemn and returned to their cars. Others sat down at the grave, clipped grass from the base of the stone or sat silent. A few cried, looking toward the heavens, their thoughts known only to themselves.

Once a grave had been dug the workers looked down into the smooth sides they had fashioned and were silent a moment before one said, "If he doesn't get to heaven, it won't be our fault. We preached him a real nice funeral while we talked."

Another worker laughed, agreeing, "We did, at that. But the preacher can do a lot better job than us amateurs." The men stepped away from the grave, putting their hands to their backs, straightened up slowly and drifted away, tools in hand.

On the way home, Dad asked if I had learned anything new. I replied that I had found a cemetery was an easier place for the dead than it was for the living. He never replied, but I'm sure he knew what I meant.

In a few years, the number of farmers in the area declined as farms grew larger. Graves were opened by back hoes and other machines operated by men unaware of whom would be buried there. And another bit of Americana faded into history.

Creek Baptisms

Most rural churches conducted baptisms in creeks in the 1930s, their baptisteries a thing of the future. Each baptism was paradoxical, a solemn event, yet a celebration of choice.

We recall one that was similar to most.

A caravan of cars, moving slowly, churned the red clay dust on the gravel road into blankets of fog. The cars stopped and a man got out, swung open the big farm gate and got back in. The caravan passed through. A passenger in the last car closed the gate.

In the cars that golden summer day were members of a rural church en route to a baptizing. The cars proceeded down a lane before turning at the banks of Back Creek, a stream that meandered down the eastern side of Lawrence County east of Heltonville. The drivers parked the cars as best they could under the cooling shade of the trees that lined the creek.

Horses in the field swished the flies from their backs with their long tails. Cows munched on the few blades of grass that were still green. The dried vegetation crackled under the feet of the congregation as it walked slowly to the creek. The members walked to the west bank to view the minister, who already waited on a sand bar. A group of youngsters in their teens stood near the preacher.

The water was clear, the sandstone bottom visible a half-fathom deep in a pool 25 feet wide and 75 feet long. It looked as big as an ocean. Beams from the sun found their way through the leaves of overhanging trees, turning the iridescent scales on the goldfish into a bright glow.

An acquaintance, who grew up in the area, later wrote us from his home in California, his memories of that day:

"My mind was more on fishing than on the baptism, but I tried not to let it show. My commitment to the Lord would come later. The congregation broke into song, 'Shall We Gather at the River.' The only accompaniment was the distant mating call of a bobwhite. The minister used a stick to steady himself and waded out into the water.

"The young women who were to be baptized followed slowly, fearfully. The boys came more quickly, yet more reluctantly, they would confess later. I made a mental note of what followed."

He was to recall in that letter five decades later: "Individually, sacredly, solemnly, the minister immersed each of the new members. Some of the faces came up from the water with an ecstatic shine. One or two gave a shout of joy."

"More hymns followed the final immersion. It was a time of celebration, an unbounded celebration to the Creator and his Son. A final prayer was said. The congregation and newly-baptized, still in wet clothes, returned to their cars and then departed as it had come."

Faubie recalled he stopped briefly to cast another look back at the scene. The water had been churned into a light-brown from the baptisms and the fish no longer could be seen. Like others he vowed, someday, to return to the scene and capture the meaning of that July day.

THE POST WAR ERA

Return to Normal

Once World War II ended the nation turned quickly from a wartime economy. Factories that retooled from the manufacture of weapons of war shifted quickly to production of goods and services for homes and individuals.

Factories that had built tanks and other arsenal slowly began to assemble cars and trucks. New refrigerators, ranges, washers and dryers returned to stores.

Given little notice outside Indianapolis was the purchase of the Indianapolis Motor Speedway by Terre Haute industrialist Anton (Tony) Hulman. The November 14, 1945, acquisition assured fans that the 500-Mile Race would continue to run throughout the century and beyond.

Men put away their military uniforms and returned to civilian clothes, some to join the 52-20 Club. Many used their GI Bill of Rights to enter colleges, changing for a time the preppy ivy towers of learning into mature institutions of serious thought.

(It was an asset for we teen-age college underclassmen to be associated with veterans who became our mentors and taught us that education was a privilege not to be taken lightly).

The World War II victory of freedom over oppressive tyranny allowed Americans to view the future with optimism. It was assumed the American way of life would prevail unchallenged. That belief was short-lived. Winston Churchill, appearing at a small Missouri college in 1946 declared that a Soviet "iron curtain" had fallen across Europe, from the Baltic to the Adriatic." Communism became a synonym for fear, that fear the belief that the Soviet Union would attempt to spread its philosophy around the globe so soon after freedom had been preserved.

That dread would rise and fall over the years to come.

And the search for independence by others continued. India had won its freedom from Great Britain in 1947, thanks to Mohandas (Mahatma) Gandhi 78, one of the first apostles of nonviolence. The assassination on January 30, 1948, was blamed on a shooter who acted for a faction that disagreed with Gandhi's stance against violence. It made, instead, the spiritual leader of millions of Hindus a martyr and set the stage for nonviolent demonstrations in America in the decades ahead.

Death came to Indiana on March 26 that year when 19 Hoosiers were killed and 200 injured by a tornado that slashed across central Indiana. Among the hardest hit towns were Coatesville, which was left in rubble, Danville and Hadley in Hendricks County.

The Red Menace

Less than a week later, communism was back in the news. The Soviet Union closed off ground-level entry into occupied Berlin from the west and required all passengers to undergo Russian inspection. The move completed the partition of the German capital into sectors, effectively dividing the city. The U.S. with the aid of England and France negated the Soviet move with one of history's greatest airlifts of food and supplies.

The fear of communism aside, the peace time economy was on an upswing as the 1948 election approached.

Truman Wins!

The presidential nominees, as expected, were President Harry Truman and Republican Tom Dewey, who had run well in a loss to President Roosevelt in 1944. A third candidate added intrigue and uncertainty to the race when the States' Rights Party chose Strom Thurmond as its candidate.

Truman flaunts erroneous headline

Truman told Hoosiers in a speech from the rear of his campaign train at Garrett, Indiana, "Former Governor (Henry) Schricker, and I are looking to see Indiana in the right column all the way down the line this time." The crisp talking president, added: "G.O.P. means Grand Old Platitudes in this day and age."

Dewey, however, was a heavy favorite to win Indiana and enough other states to regain the White House for the GOP for the first time since 1932. Even after Truman took a lead in the vote, The *Chicago Tribune* assumed late voters would change the outcome and bannered its famous "DEWEY DEFEATS TRUMAN" headline that remains a classic collector's item.

Truman had 24,179,345 or 49.6 percent of the votes and carried 31 states; Dewey 45.1 percent of the vote and 14 states, Thurmond 1,176,125 votes and three states. Truman squeezed by Dewey in Indiana, 821,074 to 807,833 votes. Thurmond was not a factor.

My dad had been no fan of President Roosevelt. He didn't really care for Truman, although he admired his down home speech and common sense. He never took to the urbane but uncharismatic Dewey, but I had assumed he would vote for the Republican. He later admitted he had chosen Truman, explaining times were good and all seemed well with the nation. Even then Americans voted with their pocketbooks. Even then polls and predictions of outcomes could be wrong.

Henry Schricker, whom Truman mentioned in his Garrett speech, had been elected governor in 1940, then, being barred at the time from two consecutive terms, ran unsuccessfully in 1944 for the U.S. Senate against Republican Homer E. Capehart. Schricker's 1948 election let him return to the statehouse for four more years.

Republican William E. Jenner of Bedford was elected to the U.S. Senate in 1944 to fill an unexpired term, then was-reelected in 1946 to a full six-year term. His election meant southern Indiana was home to both senators, Capehart being from nearby Washington.

The Arms Race

The 1940s ended as the decade had started with uncertainty around the globe. Small countries subject to imperialism sought freedom. Communism and nations like the USSR and China threatened peace.

NATO was organized to oppose the Soviet Union, which detonated its first atomic bomb signaling the start of an arms race that would continue into the 1980s. To the southeast, communists won the Chinese Civil War.

Decolonalization continued as Indonesia became free of the control of the Netherlands.

*   *   *

A new decade was ahead. In a few months, Americans would return to the battlefield, this time in Korea. The Associated Press reported in a dispatch from Seoul on June 27, 1950: "Invading North Korean communists stabbed a tank column to the outskirts of this southern repubic's capital today and demanded the surrender of South Korea."

Youths from cities and towns would soon don the military gear they were too young to wear in World War II. Once again Americans would learn that freedom is maintained only by diligence.

*   *   *

Despite how much history repeats itself, it is unlikely there will ever be two consecutive decades as historic and as momentous as the 1930s and 1940s. Those of us who were a part of them should be stronger and wiser because of them. We are grateful for having been a minuscule part of both.

Other Books By Wendell Trogdon

NOSTALGIA:

TRAVEL

BIOGRAPHY

BASKETBALL

For more information about any of these books, contact the author at P. O. Box 651, Mooresville, IN 46158-0651, call him at 317-831-2815, or send an e-mail message to wend@iquest.net.

ABOUT THE AUTHOR

With The 1930s and 1940s—Pain and Pleasure author Wendell Trogdon returns to an era he featured in his newspapers columns and his five popular *Those Were the Days* books.

Now far removed from that era, his memories remain vivid.

Families were close out of necessity, each son or daughter had a role to play be it in the home or on the farm. Neighbors exchanged work, huckster wagons delivered staples to homes and news traveled via telephone over party lines. Life was simple, movies were wholesome and radio was humorous.

This is the author's 21st book and one of his favorites. It catches the essence of a remarkable period in which the nation went from innocence to maturity, from depression to war.

Seven other of the books are about Indiana high school basketball. He is co-author of two of those with Damon Bailey, *Damon—Living A Dream,* and *Damon—Beyond the Glory.*

Some of his most popular books have been about roads: *Backroads Indiana*, a journal of his travels over unbeaten paths to small southern Indiana towns; *Borderline Indiana*, a look at the people and places on the borders of the state; *U.S. 50: From Washington to St. Louis, and Lonely is the Road*, which covers the area west from St. Louis.

Among his other titles are *Indiana General Stores/Vanishing Landmarks*, and *Main Street Diners/Where Hoosiers Start The Day.*

Trogdon retired as managing editor of *The Indianapolis News* in 1992 after a 38-year career that began as a reporter for the *Logansport Pharos-Tribune*. He has continued to write for other periodicals.

He grew up on a farm in Lawrence County, where he lived the experiences he shares in this book.

He resides at Mooresville, Indiana, with his wife Fabian, who has traveled with him on many journeys around the state and nation.